Golfing Across the Ponds
A Duffer's Perspective

Dr. George G. Kitchens

The author is a Retired Board Certified Otolaryngologist (ENT) and Facial Plastic Surgeon. He grew up in a small east-central Georgia town, Warrenton, in the shadow of Augusta, Georgia. For the last 60 years he has been enamored with golf and The Masters Tournament.

He has been married for 49 years to Faye Thompson of Milledgeville, Georgia which is located in the center of the state. They have two children Holly Kitchens Brass and G. Gray Kitchens, Jr. The loves of his life are his five grandchildren: Ava Gray Kitchens, Benjamin Matthew Brass, Mary Lily Thompson Brass, Kathryn (Kate) Grace Kitchens, and Lila Jane Kitchens.

He has traveled extensively in the USA and abroad, played 541 different courses in 26 states and 14 other countries. His travel has taken him to Scotland 7 times, Ireland 6 times, and England 3 times for golf. These experiences have motivated him to share his travel ideas with others.

For the last 30 years he has kept an ever-expanding list of his favorite courses. Rather than use a strict criteria for this ranking, the only real buzzword is the 'ambience' the course and club radiate. Certainly reputation, esthetics, conditioning and scenery play a role, but in the end, it is only the opinion of the author on which courses to include in this list. (See List of Favorites)

He is a member of Wade Hampton Golf Club, The Country Club of Sapphire Valley both in Cashiers, NC and Greenville County Club, Greenville, SC. His other hobbies include blue water sailing, playing the bagpipes, singing second tenor, travel and reading. In the summer he and his wife live in Cashiers, NC, in the winter in Greenville, SC. The author can be contacted at georgegkitchens27@gmail.com.

Cover photograph of Royal County Down Golf Club, Newcastle, Northern Ireland

Foreword
Tom Fazio

I have been in the golf business almost all of my life and I have been designing golf courses for over fifty years. During that time I have traveled millions of miles; I have toured hundreds of potential golf course sites; I have designed over 200 golf courses throughout the United States and abroad, and I have been blessed to play quite a bit of golf throughout my life and career. I can say without hesitation that George Kitchens has seen and experienced infinitely more golf around the world than I ever will, and this book is a glimpse into the fascinating and diverse world of golf that so many of us enjoy, but will simply never have the opportunity to experience in such a comprehensive way. George takes the reader along with him on his many travels, offering insights into travel planning and golf course recommendations as well as humorous "off the course" asides and stories that can often make for memories as precious as the golf itself.

George Kitchens has been a friend for many years now thanks to our mutual affiliation with and enjoyment of Wade Hampton Golf Club in Cashiers, North Carolina, a golf course I designed in the late 1980's and which currently enjoys a ranking by Golf Digest as the #1 course in North Carolina. I have enjoyed spending time over the last 30 years at Wade Hampton and I certainly have some very fond memories of George over that time. He is a dedicated husband and father and a doting grandfather. This book is his labor of love and I hope you enjoy the stories in the pages ahead.

Tom Fazio

Preface
Judge Ian Bamford

(Past President Golfing Union of Ireland and former
Irish Open Amateur Golf Champion)

I was very pleased when the author invited me to
write a preface to this book. I share his enthusiasm
for the game of golf and value our longstanding and
respected friendship. This friendship goes back to the
very early 1990's, when a group of golfers from
"Wade Hampton Golf Club, North Carolina," visited
Ireland and most fittingly our paths first crossed at the
magnificent links of "Royal County Down Golf Club,
Newcastle, County Down", where I and some other
members of that club were pleased to host and play
with the Wade Hampton party. This group included
many from our "Walker Cup" match at Peachtree,
Atlanta, including my friend Tom Dowden.

Dr. George was called upon to tell a few stories,
which he did in his inimitable southern drawl and the
party began, aided by a few shots of Irish Whiskey
and the comforts of the Slieve Donard Hotel, which
sits right beside the renowned links of Royal County
Down.

I did say that our friendship was a respected one:
having read his book I realize that the author has
played many more golf links and courses than I have
and has taken the time and trouble to write about
them and also to rank them. I urge you to read his
book which covers courses not only in the southern

hemisphere but in Ireland, Scotland and the Continent of Europe.

Dr. George provides some good tips for fitting in many rounds of golf on quality courses in seven or eight days; he writes from experience and writes wisely.

As I pin this preface the 41st Ryder Cup has concluded at "Hazeltine National Golf Club, Minnesota" and I salute the skill and determination of the USA team, so well captained by Davis Love III, resulting in a win by 17-11 for team USA. Well done to the USA; as this course is now truly famous, can we expect the author to add it to his impressive list of 541 courses played in 15 different countries and 26 different USA states?

Ian Bamford
09/11/16

Golfing Across The Ponds
A Duffer's Perspective

Table of Contents

Becoming a Favorite 7
List of Favorite Courses 9
Introduction to Traveling 17
Chapter I Scotland 19
    Part I The East 20
    Part II The North 40
    Part III The West 52
Chapter II Ireland 70
    Part I Dublin & Northern Ireland 72
    Part II The North-West Irish Republic 86
    Part III The South-West Irish Republic 96
Chapter III England 110
    Part I The South of London and Surry 111
    Part II The North-West of England 122
Chapter IV Europe 139
    Part I Portugal 140
    Part II The Rhine River Valley 147
Chapter V The Caribbean 155
    Part I Bermuda 156
    Part II The Bahamas 158
    Part III Cuba 168
    Part IV Jamaica 173
    Part V The Dominican Republic 175
    Part VI St. Maarten 184
Chapter VI Mexico 187
Chapter VII New Zealand 204
Chapter VIII Australia 220
    Part I Tasmania 223
    Part II Melbourne 228
    Part III Adelaide and Sydney 244

Becoming a Favorite

For my fortieth birthday in 1984, my brother, C. Ralph Kitchens, Jr. arranged for me to play Augusta National Golf Club. I should mention that I started going to the Masters in 1958 when I was fourteen and have not missed a Masters Tournament since. I recognized early on that this event was very special, with impeccable organization, it was destined for greatness. That's why in 2018 I will be attending my sixty-first straight tournament in the last sixty years.

But back to that birthday round; it was a dream come true for me. I couldn't stop talking about it and in the operating room the next week I commented: "That might be as close to heaven as I ever get". The scrub nurse in the next instant said: "That's a fact". Her worldly insight into my personality is what triggered my thinking about a list of celestial favorites. Playing these 125 courses is like my personal stairway to heaven. Why 125 courses and not more or less? After I had counted all the courses I had played in early 2013, my list of favorites was composed of courses played since 1984 and was approximately 75-80 venues. I went back to the list of all courses played and selected those I thought were worthy of being included in my list. I quickly got over 100 and finally settled on capping the list at 125. My list is not static, but ever changing, as I find one that is definitely deserving, I delete one.

The ambience the course and club radiate is my heavenly criteria, but its hard for me to put into words exactly what I like after that initial impression. Here are some terrestrial things I like: links courses with great views of the ocean from close and elevated bluffs: these courses allow one to chip or putt with run up shots rather than fly the ball to the pin. Let's face it, duffers like myself cannot spin the ball. I'm pleased when playing courses that require analysis and a strategic plan with what route to play from tee to green, depending on one's ability: I like to play forward, but still get the true flavor and experience of the course. The difficulty in obtaining an invitation to play a certain course is a factor, as is the exclusivity of its membership. Esthetics and conditioning go a long way with me, but I must admit to being a golf snob: when choosing a course I opt for highly rated ones. But when ranking a course, well then, I revert to plain old me. This paragraph attempts to tell why I like a course, but along the way I will try to relay why I don't list a certain course.

Why the subtitle "A Duffer's Perspective"? Well I am not a rater with a single digit handicap. The lowest my handicap has ever been is thirteen after my two years in the United States Air Force and yet still a young man. So I'm not masquerading as an authority of how to play the game, as a golf course architect or as a golf historian. I simply love the game; being outside with friends, match play competition, and small wagers. I'm constantly struggling to improve my current index of around twenty, but happy with whatever I shoot. Other than otolaryngology and facial surgery the only other thing I feel very knowledgeable about is golf travel and the great courses around the world. So, I decided, in contrast to the golf writers and architects who usually write about new venues and places to play, I would write this book and give the reader "A Duffer's Perspective".

Favorite Courses as of January 2017

1, Augusta National Golf Club

2. Pine Valley Golf Club

3. Cypress Point Golf Club

4. Royal County Down Golf Club

5. Shinnecock Hills Golf Club

6. The Honourable Company cf Edinburg Golfers at Muirfield

7. The National Golf Links of America

8. Chicago Golf Club

9. Royal Dornoch Golf Club

10. Royal Melbourne Golf Club (West Course)

11. Wade Hampton Golf Club

12. Trump Turnberry (Ailsa Course)

13. Seminole Golf Club

14. Royal Portrush Golf Club

15. Cape Kidnappers

16. Old Course St. Andrews

Favorites Page 2

17. San Francisco Golf Club

18. Kauri Cliffs

19. Pebble Beach Golf Links

20. Estancia Club

21. Sand Hills Golf Club

22. Kingsbarns Golf Club

23. Monterey Peninsula CC (Shore Course)

24. Olympic Club (Lake Course)

25. Barnbougle Dunes Golf Club

26. Alotian Club

27. Carne Golf Club

28. Quaker Ridge Golf Club

29. The Quarry at La Quinta

30. Bandon Dunes Golf Course

31. Baltusrol Golf Club (Lower Course)

32. Cruden Bay Golf Club

33. Pinehurst # 2

Favorites Page 3

34. Medinah III Golf Course

35. Castle Stuart Golf Club

36. Pacific Dunes Golf Course

37. Maidstone Golf Club

38. Spyglass Hill Golf Club

39. Lahinch Golf Club

40. Yeamans Hall Club

41. The Country Club of Brookline

42. Royal Troon Golf Club

43. Indian Creek Country Club

44. Jupiter Hills (Hills Course)

45. Whistling Straits (Straits Course)

46. Kinloch Golf Club

47. Kingston Heath Golf Club

48. Kiawah Island Club (River Course)

49. Pablo Creek Golf Club

50. Secession Golf Club

Favorites Page 4

51. Shadow Creek Golf Club

52. Querencia Golf Club

53. Sea Island Golf Club (Seaside Course)

54. Sunningdale Golf Club (Old Course)

55. Cap Cana Resort (Punta Espada Course)

56. Ocean Forest Golf Club

57. Bighorn Club (Canyon Course)

58. Peachtree Golf Club

59. The Renaissance Club

60. Frederica Golf Club

61. Royal Aberdeen Golf Club

62. Cabo de Sol (Ocean Course)

63. Royal Birkdale Golf Club

64. Fallen Oak Golf Club

65. Machrihanish Dunes Golf Club

66. Corales Golf Club

67. Rosses Point Golf Club (County Sligo)

Favorites Page 5

68. Burning Tree

69. Palmetto Golf Club, Aiken, SC

70. Whisper Rock (Lower Course)

71. Enniscrone Golf Club (Dunes Course)

72. Harbor Town Golf Links

73. Ballybunion Golf Club (Old Course)

74. Shoreacres Golf Club

75. Bay Hill Club

76. Western Gailes Golf Club

77. Mid Ocean Club

78. Blackwolf Run (River Course)

79. Kiawah Island Club (Cassique Course)

80. Medalist Golf Club

81. Greenville Country Club (Chanticleer Course)

82. Baltusrol Golf Club (Upper Course)

83. Biltmore Forest Golf Club

84. The Victoria Golf Club, Melbourne

Favorites Page 6

85. Diamante Golf Club (Dunes Course)

86. Camp Creek Golf Club

87. North Berwick (West Links)

88. Atlanta Athletic Club (Highlands Course)

89. Sage Valley Golf Club

90. Mountain Brook Country Club

91. Black Diamond Ranch Golf and Country Club (The Quarry Course)

92. East Lake Golf Club

93. Portmarnock Golf Club

94. Royal Liverpool Golf Club (Hoylake)

95. Waterville Golf Club

96. The Golf Club at Cuscowilla

97. New South Wales Golf Club

98. Islesworth Golf Club

99. Wentworth (West Course)

100. Country Club of Birmingham (West Course)

101. Whisper Rock (Upper Course)

Favorites Page 7

102. Highlands Country Club

103. Ballyliffin Golf Club (Glashedy Links)

104. Timuquana Country Club

105. Torrey Pines Golf Club (South Course)

106. TPC Sawgrass (Stadium Course)

107. Caso de Campo, Dominican Republic

108. The Homestead (Cascades Upper Course}

109. Augusta Country Club

110. Shoal Creek Golf and Country Club

111. Champions Retreat Golf Club, Augusta, GA

112. The Country Club of Sapphire Valley

113. Mirabel Golf Club

114. Country Club of Virginia (James River Course)

115. Kiva Dunes Golf Club, Gulf Shores, AL

116. Olympia Fields (North Course)

117. Montgomery Country Club

118. Ponte Vedra Club (Ocean Course)

Favorites Page 8

119. Mauna Kea Golf Club (Resort Course)

120. Macrihanish Golf Club

121. Walton Heath Golf Club

122. Belle Mead Country Club (Nashville TN)

123. The Carnegie Club at Skibo Castle

124. Royal Lytham & St. Annes Golf Club

125. Ventana Canyon (Mountain Course)

Introduction to Traveling

The term "across the pond" has been used for decades to describe traveling from the United States to the United Kingdom and Ireland to play golf. If the Atlantic is one pond, I am simply adding the Caribbean Sea, The Sea of Cortez, The Gulf of Mexico and the granddaddy pond of them all, the Pacific Ocean, to describe my travels for golf and exploring.

First, there are several generalities regarding travel to the UK. Plan way ahead! Some of the "Must Play" courses I will discuss take tee times a year in advance, and if you wait to make reservations you will miss out. I would not travel earlier than early May or later than late October. Plan for any type of weather: a good waterproof rain suit is a must, with layers of capline or similar fabric, cotton or wool turtle- necks and both wool and cotton sweaters. A sports jacket and tie is needed at some of the old clubs, especially if you are planning to have lunch. The Scots and Irish have developed lunch to an art form so do not miss out!

Having said that, the old adage, "when traveling across the pond take half as much clothing and twice as much money" is good advice. Most of the flights from the US to the UK leave late afternoon or at night. Conversely, coming back they tend to leave in the morning for a late afternoon arrival back home. Unless you have time to spare or, don't mind missing one day going or returning, arrive at your gateway city 12-24 hours before departure across the Ponds.

"Jet Lag"- what's that? Let's face it: you are pumped and excited to be going, so you probably will not sleep well even in the new bed type seats. Have a couple of drinks, beers or wine with dinner. Eat as soon as you can on the plane: no drawn out meals in business class. Then take a sleep aid; personally I take tylenol pm, Benadryl, or a prescribed sleep aid. Try to get four or five hours sleep on the plane, drink lots of water before, during and after the flight and move around, walk the aisle and stand in the galley.

1. Customs: It's usually not a problem, so I would advise playing the day you get there, provided the course is within 90 minutes of the airport. Give yourself two hours to clear customs, get your luggage and obtain a rental car or van.

2. Trip organization and reservations: If it's your first time you will need a golf travel agent to make the arrangements, but don't take their recommendations for courses at face value: TAKE MINE! Have your itinerary well planned out before you phone them, as I will discuss.

3. Car rental: For groups of four or less you probably can drive yourself if: 1. You have a designated driver not drinking that day and 2. you have someone in the group who has driven in the UK previously. It's really not hard to get accustomed to driving on the left side. For groups of more that four that require a bigger vehicle, an agent is a must. My recommendations are to interview several and get quotes. Kalos Golf is good, but high end. For travel to Ireland, Carr Golf is a good bet. Lastly, have $20 or so changed at the airport to pounds for the UK, Euros for the Republic of Ireland and local currency for others. Take a debit card and get the major money you will need from an ATM there. Do not try to pay with dollars!

Chapter I

Scotland

It's only logical to start this book with Scotland, the birthplace of golf as we know it, and the country that I'm most familiar with. Having traveled to both Scotland and Ireland multiple times, I am frequently asked which country is best or which one to visit first. I really cannot answer that question any other way but to say both. I suppose if you want more golf history I would say Scotland. On the other hand if you just want good golf courses maybe, and I do mean maybe, Ireland is slightly better. They are both wonderful.

Indeed you cannot do justice to either country with just one visit. I divide Scotland into three distinct areas. Those three area are: first the east, Edinburgh and environs, to include St. Andrews, second the north of Scotland, and thirdly the west of Scotland. (Figure 1) You really need one visit to each of these three areas to cover it all, and there are one or two must play courses in each area.

So let's start with Edinburgh, which has plenty of direct flights from all major US cities. I may mention courses in different areas, but the ones that I will discuss at length, I have played, many of them multiple times. My suggestion is to start in East Lothian, fly over on a Saturday or Sunday, play a less famous course (close to Muirfield) on a Monday in East Lothian, and play Muirfield on a Tuesday.

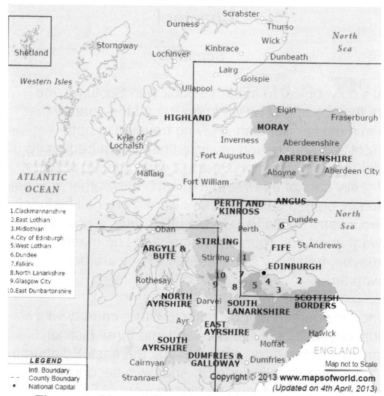

Figure 1. Map of Scotland with the three areas outlined

Part I
The East

Muirfield: Home of The Honourable Company of Edinburgh Golfers, East Lothian, Scotland

This is the first must play course in the East Scotland area. It's my favorite in Scotland and highest on my list of favorites there at sixth. I've played it nine times, five of which were in Scotch Foursomes matches. The first among many rules is that the Club takes guests for unaccompanied play on Tuesdays and

Thursdays only. Plan your trip to the east area so that you have a full day here. Trust me, a day is not enough to absorb all that is here. First and foremost it has the reputation of being very stuffy and unyielding and denying access to anyone who has not made prior arrangments, even well known golf architects or players.

So book at least a year in advance on the internet. hceg@muirfield.org.uk or 011 44 1620 842123. The Honourable Company of Edinburgh Golfers, hence-forth referred to as HCEG, play almost exclusively Scotch Foursomes or alternate shot. They do this because during winter play it's only light for 6-7 hours. The foursome matches go very quickly, 2- 21/2 hours each. That way they have at least 2-3 hours for eating and mainly drinking. On the guest days you can play a 2,3, or a fourball off number 10 tee early morning, come into the clubhouse, change into a coat and tie and be ready for one of the best meals you will ever eat. Starting with cocktails, have claret or white wine with lunch, then top it off with an after lunch cordial and/or a cigar, before going out for a foursome match. It's the most fun a golfer can have out of bed.

The Secretary once told the new club Manager that The HCEG was "really a lunch club that just happened to be located on a really good golf course". Muirfield is the third site occupied by the HCEG; they published the rules of golf in 1744. As such it is the oldest formally organized golf club in the world.

The first course, occupied in 1744, was located in Leith. The HCEG later moved to the Old Course in Musselburgh. Its nine holes are still active inside a race track. Finally in 1891 the HCEG commissioned

Old Tom Morris to lay out the present course. Fifty five miles from Edinburgh, it is hard by The Firth of Forth. The routing is brilliantly designed by Harry Colt with the outgoing nine rotating around the property in a clockwise direction. The incoming nine lies within the first and rotates in a counterclockwise direction, thereby giving the golfer the benefit of playing the constant wind in all possible directions. The entire property is enclosed in a waist high stone wall. (Figure 2)

Figure 2. The fifteenth hole at Muirfield with the second in background, inside the stone wall

The course is a magnificent piece of links land just by the Firth of Forth. The bunkers are reported to be some of the best in the world, so too are the three par fives. The uphill par 3 13th is to me one of the most memorable holes as it requires an accurate blind shot to an amphitheater green; otherwise you have an impossible shot out of severe sloping bunkers. This hole was designed by the eccentric British architect,

Tom Simpson. Why rank this course so highly? Any view toward the Firth of Forth gives one magnificent views of links land and the waving heather blowing in the constant breeze. (Figure 3)

Figure 3. The twelfth hole at Muirfield looking northeast with the Firth of Forth to the left and the Renaissance Club behind the trees to the right

I was very fortunate to play Muirfield on my second trip to Scotland in 1992. I had a temporary member-ship for 48 hours at the R&A Clubhouse. I had played my first round on The Old Course, (described in the narrative on The Old Course), and finished my second round, on the second day, at one pm. I changed into a coat and tie, had a great lunch, and was sitting in the great room watching the members looking out the famous bay windows and betting on who on the first tee would whiff the ball. A gentleman approached me: it was Dr. David Greenhough, a family physician and brother of Peter Greenhough, a former Captain of the R&A. He had seen my name and title, M.D., on the bulletin board, introduced himself and bought me a glass of port.

He was interested in my itinerary, which included three straight days at The Old Course, Gleneagles and Turnberry's Ailsa. I explained that I had researched the three best courses in Scotland and had wanted to play Muirfield but the Open was being held there in 6-8 weeks and they were not accepting guest play. He then informed me that as a member of The HCEG, he was inviting me to be his guest at Muirfield and that he had nothing on his calendar for Saturday. Well I jumped at the chance to do this, as I will admit to being a golf whore, taking any and every advantage to play all famous courses.

To say that Saturday was one of the best golfing experiences of my life would be an understatement. Dr. Greeenhough picked me up at the Caledonia Hotel at seven am and drove to Muirfield. We went into the dining rooms had 2-3 drinks and went out as a foursome (alternate shot), with David and I winning the first match on eighteen. We then changed into coat and tie, had pre-lunch cocktails, met and ate with our afternoon opponents, the four of us sharing two bottles of wine. We then retired to the smoking room where we all had an after lunch cordial, Kummel. They push that white liquor on you until it's running out of your ears. I finally said that if I had anything else to drink I will not be able to see the ball.

All in all we played thirty three holes in four hours and 58 minutes with David and I having been closed out after 15th when I triple bogeyed the par three fifteen with a shot. We came in, showered and without having anything else to drink, drove to Gleneagles. (Please see comments regarding my arrival there).

Thus began a great friendship that had me returning to Scotland, Muirfield, and visiting Dr. Greenhough in 1997, 1999, 2006 and most recently in 2011. In 1997 my close friend, Dr. Dick Vann, accompanied me. Dr. Greenhough picked us up at the Edinburgh airport and drove on to Muirfield where we stayed at Greywalls, ate a wonderful dinner at Chez Roux and partied until the wee hours at another member's summer cottage one block from the clubhouse. Dr. Vann later commented that instead of working on his golf game in preparation for playing Muirfield he should have worked more on his drinking to prepare his liver for what was to come!

North Berwick West Links, East Lothian

This is a good course to book on the arrival day. It's 2 miles west of Muirfield, some 57 miles from the Edin-burgh airport. I played this course on my first trip to Scotland some 31-32 years ago and again in 2003. It's most famous for the original Redan hole #15. The other unique hole is the 13th, "The Pit", that plays over a short stone fence. It's right on the Firth of Forth with beautiful views of the water. Six holes are directly by the ocean which come into play at high tide.

The modern course was designed by David Strath in 1878. However, allegedly golf has been played here since the 17th century and the Club was formed in 1832. Tom Doak has it in his Gourmet's list in "The Confidential Guide to Golf Courses" so you cannot go wrong playing it. Also the town of North Berwick has several hotels and restaurants which face the golf course. In my list of favorites, I have it at 87. When we visited it in the early 1980's, my son Gray, then nine, played along side me with a pull cart. The crusty old caddie wouldn't touch his bag and I ended up pulling it around the course. I got the idea that this traditional old guy felt that a nine year old had no business playing his famous old course.

The Renaissance Club, East Lothian

This Course, directly adjacent to Muirfield's east, opened in 2008 to rave reviews. It's designed by Tom Doak in his minimalistic style and serves the magnificent setting perfectly. It's a private club which caters to every need of its international membership. When I went in 2011, arrangements were made through connections I have in Augusta and my tour agent. Again the Firth of Forth is a dominant landmark, but in contrast to Muirfield, this Club sits high above the Firth of Forth, affording the golfer magnificent views. There is not a weak hole on the outgoing nine.

The incoming nine, beginning with a difficult dogleg right tenth, is undergoing revision placing the holes closer to the beach and The Firth of Forth. It's on the old Archerfield estate, close to another new course by that name that I haven't played. I have it fifty-seventh in my favorites list and would recommend playing it if possible. (Figure 4)

We almost missed playing here because our plane was grounded in Charlotte with connections through

Newark. Thank the Lord that US Airways had another flight to Edinburgh that night. The reason was that Obama had flown into New Jersey to inspect the

Figure 4. The Renaissance Club with number sixteen in the foreground, twelve in the middle and The Firth of Forth in the background

hurricane damage on the New Jersey coast, holding up air traffic for four hours. Little did we know that the hurricane would impact our travels over a week later.

Others in East Lothian:
Archerfield Golf Links is a private club very close to the three courses I have played here. The Fidra Course was designed by David (D.J.) Russell, a European tour professional, in 2004. On the map it looks slightly inland from the Firth of Forth. According to their website, the links aspect comes into play from the 12th hole onward. The second course at

Archerfield, also designed by Mr. Russell, Dirleton, recently opened and it's definitely further inland.

Gulliane Numbers 1,2, and 3 are closer to Edinburgh. Number 1 is the oldest (1884) and probably the best as it has hosted numerous national and international tournaments, most recently the 2015 Aberdeen Asset Management Scottish Open. Sixteen holes from number 1 and two holes from number 2 were used for the 2015 tournament. Both number 2 and 3 were designed by Willie Park, Jr. in 1898 and 1910 respectively. Number 3 is noticeably shorter and probably good for shorter hitters like myself. Either of these three is a good site to play on your arrival day.

I've already mentioned Musselburgh as the second home of HCEG. It's a nine hole course, still open, which has not changed in over 150 years. It is still located in the center of a horse racetrack, but not associated with the HCEG and would be another alternative to North Berwick upon arrival in Scotland.

We haven't talked about playing more than one round a day. Other than at Muirfield, I have rarely played over 18 holes per day. All the courses in East Lothian and Fife are close enough to one another so that it is easy to play two on some of the days of your trip. Considering it's light for 18-20 hours a day in the summer, you may want to do that, but again plan way ahead.

St. Andrews Links Trust, located in the town of St. Andrews, Fife, Scotland is a charitable organization owned by the citizens of St. Andrews. It consists of seven courses which are public. In alphabetical order they are:

1. Balgove Course, a nine hole course built on Balgove farm in 1972
2. Castle Course, opened in 2008, the youngest
3. Eden Course, opened in 1914
4. Jubilee Course, the longest, opened in 1897
5. Strathtyrum, named after the estate that it was built on in 1993, the second youngest course
6. The Old Course, the oldest course in the world and on which golf has been played since the early fourteen hundreds
7. The New Course, not so new as it was designed by Old Tom Morris in 1895.

The town of St. Andrews, Fife, Scotland lies on the northern shore of the peninsula of Fife on St. Andrews Bay. It's approximately 75 miles north of Edinburgh. You cross the magnificent Firth of Forth Bridge on the way. The town is beautiful, full of the old ruins of the cathedral, (Figure 5) pubs, restaurants, hotels and most importantly, golf courses. The Royal and Ancient Clubhouse sits in the center of town on the first tee of The Old Course. Previously, a member of the R&A could recommend a temporary membership, good for a two day visit to the clubhouse. Today, however that member or a member must be present for you to enter. Again, I hate to recommend hotels or restaurants, but if price is no object, The Old Course Hotel is great. At the very least have a drink in the top floor bar overlooking The Old and New Courses. The Dunvegan Hotel has the best bar in town, and is not a bad place to stay as well. The last time. we stayed up the street at the Ardgowan Hotel which is also nice. The St. Andrews links clubhouse, with its Swilcan restaurant across the street from the Old Course's 18th fairway, serves the Old, New and Jubilee Courses.

Figure 5. Ruins of St. Andrews Cathedral

The Old Course, St. Andrews, Fife, Scotland

What can I say about The Old Course that has not
been said before? It's the "Home of Golf" and the
second must play course in the East Scotland region.
It's mind boggling to realize that golf has been played
on this ground since the 1400's. That's 600 years ago
and 100 or so years before Henry VIII became King of
England! No golf trip to Scotland would be complete
skipping this course. The bunkers were not built by
man; rather they were hollowed out by sheep
burrowing down in the ground to avoid the fierce wind
off the Bay of St. Andrews. Only the first, ninth,
seventeenth and eighteenth greens are single; the
others are huge, double greens, whose numbers all

add up to 18. (Figure 6) The Club and Course were formally established in 1552.

My first round here is one of my most memorable ever. I had a guest membership for 48 hours and because of that was able to find a match with Stuart Larson, a member of the R&A as well as Augusta National, and with P.J. Boatwright Jr. and his new wife. Our tee time was 5:10pm. I remember thinking and asking if we could finish before darkness whereupon the starter looked at me astounded and informed me that darkness would fall slightly after midnight. The new Mrs. Boatwright and Mr. Larson beat us 3 & 2, as I recall.

In contrast to the above wonderful first experience with "The Old", two of golf's most famous players had less than a pleasant experience their first time here. Bobby Jones, playing in his first Open in 1921, hit in the very deep Hill Bunker fronting the eleventh hole during his third round. (Figure 7) After taking four shots in the bunker, he picked his ball up and tore up his score card, officially withdrawing from the tournament. It's interesting to note that after he apparently calmed down, he finished both his third and fourth rounds at The Old Course, but firmly stated his dislike of it. This too changed, as by the time he won the 1927 Open here, he was relating how much he liked it. That year he further endeared himself to the people of the UK by letting the trophy stay in the R&A Clubhouse, rather than taking it home for the year. He won the British Amateur here in 1930, the year of his historic Grand Slam. As further testimony

Figure 6. The sixteenth hole at St. Andrews Old
Course with number two in background

of the mutual respect, Jones was named a Freeman
of the City of St. Andrews in 1958. Benjamin Franklin
is the only other American so honored.

In 1946 the Open Championship was held, for the first
time since 1939, at The Old Course St. Andrews.
Sam Snead won his only Open Championship here
by four strokes. When asked what he thought of the
course he said: "It looks like an old abandoned kinda
place." Needless to say the caustic British press had
a field day over both these slights to their beloved Old
Course. Snead played in the 1937 Open and three
other times in the early 1960's, but never won again.

Figure 7. Number eleven of The Old Course with the
Hill Bunker shown and the Eden Estuary
in the background

You can book a tee time over the internet, but must
book another round on one of the other Links Trust
courses also. It's probably more reliable to use a golf
travel agent to arrange your round well in advance. If
you are there and do not have a time, there is a ballot
which you can sign up for two days in advance and
maybe you'll get a starting time. If all else fails, a
single can frequently get out, as I did in 1992, but only
after a couple of hours waiting. One other piece of
advice: your first time playing this course GET A
CADDIE. There are a tremendous number of blind
tee or approach shots and to attempt to navigate this
course on your own is like sailing from Key West to
Havana without any navigational aids!

Oh, by the way, I've had this course ranked in the top ten of my favorites, but as I played other good courses, it crept up to twenty-three or so. As I analyzed this list recently, I have placed it at sixteen.

Eden Course, St. Andrews, Fife Scotland

Much more forgiving than the other three courses and closer to the Bay of St. Andrews, The Eden is directly adjacent to the inward nine of The Old Course. It was designed and built by Harry S. Colt in 1914 and named for the estuary which is one of the natural boundaries defining this links course. It is a 6,200+ yards course with a par of 70. The Eden Course was one of the first, if not the first, that Alister MacKenzie helped Mr. Colt design. I played it on a sightseeing/ golf trip with my family to London and Edinburgh in 1983. My son Gray, then 9, and I drove up to play at St. Andrews. As the Old Course was closed for maintenance in March, they suggested we play The Eden. We rented a car and a block out from Hertz two mirrors, one on our car and one on a parked car were the first casual- ties of me driving on the left. I told Gray if he told his mother I would kill him, and we laughed all the way.

When we got to St. Andrews, it was 2:05 pm and all the restaurants were closed. It seemed that it was too late for lunch and too early for dinner. The only thing we could find to eat were cheese crackers and a coke or a beer. Boy, how St. Andrews has changed since 1983. I had a caddie and Gray a pull cart that I pulled most of the round, as the caddie wouldn't touch it. The only thing he helped Gray with was where to hit his putts. Gray, as I recall, had 10 one putt greens; he was sinking putts from everywhere as he hit it where the old caddie pointed to. At the end of the round, the caddie remarked that it was the best damn round of putting he had ever seen.

The New Course, St. Andrews, Fife Scotland

It's the oldest course in the world designated "New". It was commissioned by the R&A as the second course at St. Andrews in 1895, designed and built by Old Tom Morris, who at the time was Keeper of the Green at St. Andrews. We found the course very difficult and demanding from the middle tees at 6,362 yards. It's a par 71 composed of undulating fairways and challenging greens. It's on the estuary with good views of the Bay of St. Andrews and many good golfers consider it a classic test, but I wouldn't opt to play it again. When the aforementioned Dick Vann and I finished playing it, our wives had to practically carry us back to the Old Course Hotel, send us to bed, and order room service for themselves. I don't have it on my list of favorites because of its difficulty.

The Castle Course, St. Andrews, Fife Scotland

Set on a rugged cliff high above St. Andrews Bay and The North Sea just east of the town, the views here are spectacular and in my opinion that's enough, but others give mixed reviews. I haven't talked to a Scotsman who likes it, but many people do including my friend Judge Bamford (Ian Bamford is the past President of the Golfing Union of Ireland and Past Captain of Royal Portrush) with whom I had the pleasure of playing this course along with his lovely wife, Rosemary, in 2011.

The first five holes of The Castle Course are directly along the coast before it turns slightly inland. Still, one can see the Bay from them. The Course returns to the high cliffs at fourteen all the way in to the good finishing hole. Many people feel the massive green complexes are too difficult and cannot be accurately accessed and therefore are unfair. I agree so it's not in my list of favorites, but the views are to die for. (Figure 8)

Figure 8. The third hole at The Castle Course with Angus' coastland and Carnoustie in the background

Kingsbarns Golf Links, St. Andrews, Fife, Scotland

In my opinion, this is the best modern course in the UK and Ireland. I have it listed as twenty-second on my list of favorites. Developed and co-designed by Mark Parsinnen and architect Kyle Phillips in 2000, it's one not to be missed. Historically speaking, golf has been played on this site since 1793 when the Kingsbarns Golfing Society was established as the eleventh oldest golfing group. This society was rec-constituted in 1922 when Willie Auchterlonie laid out a new nine hole course.

The course is built high above the North Sea, seven miles southeast of St. Andrews. The layout is great, with the 2nd, (Figure 9), 3rd, 12th, 15th, 16th, 17th and 18th hard by the North Sea. The remaining holes are one or two fairways away from the ocean and all

Figure 9. The second hole at Kingsbarns with the North Sea in the background

have great views of it. When I first played it in July 2005 with my friend Dr. Vann from Montgomery, AL, the temperature was under 50, it was raining lightly and the wind was blowing 10-15 MPH. The first three holes were downwind and when we turned back into the wind on the fourth tee, the starter was waiting in an enclosed cart ready to take us in. I just know he thought that these two good old boys from the South couldn't take all three elements, but we could and did, the reason being is that Dr. Vann and I play in this type of weather in the Montgomery winters. I would always remark, on a miserable day, that it was just good practice for playing in Scotland and Ireland. Remember this when you want to cancel on a bad day here in the States. Why more pros do not do this type of practice is beyond my comprehension.

Other courses of note here:

Just southeast of Kingsbarns on the very tip of Fife is Crail or The Balcomie Links Course. I hear good things about it but have not taken the time to play it. I have since learned that Gil Hanse's first solo design is here, Craighead Links which opened in 1998. Now there is no reason not to try this one-two punch on the tip of Fife.
The Dukes Golf Course is slightly inland from St. Andrews, but I like to play on typical links land when in Scotland and Ireland, so I have not seen it.

The wonderful resort of Gleneagles is some 50 miles due west inland from St. Andrews. I've stayed at the magnificent hotel here, but not played the courses. After I had checked in on a trip in the late 1980's, I ran into a good friend from Montgomery on the elevator. Thank God we both had our wives with us and enjoyed a great meal together that night. The Kings and Queens courses here were both designed by James Braid. Jack Nicklaus was starting his work constructing the third course, Centenary, when we visited. I'm quoting my friend Judge Bamford who was fond of saying: "why travel to Scotland or Ireland to play a Jack Nicklaus course when there are at least 250 of them in the States or in the western hemisphere?"

The Fairmont Resort at St. Andrews along with its two eighteen holes opened in 2001. The hotel is beautiful, but the courses are a little suspect. The Torrance Course, designed by Sam Torrance, has already undergone an extensive renovation. The Kiddocks Course, designed by Bruce Devlin and Gary Stephens, is hard by the Eden Estuary affording great views of the estuary and North Sea. If you were playing in just the St. Andrews area and wanted a luxury hotel, without traveling anywhere other than St. Andrews, then this is for you.

Carnoustie Golf Links

Fifty miles around the Bay of St. Andrews, or five miles as the crow flies north of St. Andrews, is Carnoustie. Many people, because of its difficulty, call it 'Carnasty'. It's been on the Open Championship rota since 1931, hosting eight Opens, two Senior Opens and a Womens Open. Apparently golf has been played here since the middle of the fifteenth century. Nine holes of the current course were designed in 1850 by Alan Robertson of St. Andrews, and some twenty years later, Old Tom Morris extended it to eighteen holes. In 1926, James Braid redesigned the Championship course to rave reviews. Finally between The Open Championships of 1931 and 1937, James Wright of Carnoustie redesigned the last three diabolical holes with the Barry Burn running across the seventeenth and eighteenth fairways.

Probably the two most famous Opens held here were in 1953 and 1999. In 1953, Ben Hogan won his first and only Open Championship. In doing so he renamed the long, hard sixth hole "Hogan's Alley" because he was the only player to negotiate that hole which he did with a long iron to avoid the out-of-bounds which runs the length of the hole. Every living golfer may remember Jean Van de Velde's meltdown on the eighteenth and final hole in 1999. I happened to be present in the R&A's hospitality pavilion watching on a giant screen. One very British lady, with an accent to match, said: "no one other than a Frenchman could or would do that."

I returned six years later to play it, my first and last time. Carnoustie is just too hard for me along with several others I will name along the way. I was fine playing the first and the sixth, so too the final three so immortalized on TV. But both times I walked this course the rough was so high that your legs were physically beat by the time you had walked around at the tournament or finished playing it. For these reasons, I do not count Carnoustie in my list of favorites.

Part II
The North

Royal Aberdeen, Balgownie Links. Aberdeenshire, Scotland

Continuing to move north from Carnoustie, although there are several lesser known courses, the first good course you encounter is Royal Aberdeen. Currently it is sixty one on my list of favorites. I would advise one not to miss it, (maybe on your day of arrival), especially if you are flying straight into Aberdeen. Golf has been played here since 1589 with The Society of Golfers at Aberdeen founded in 1780.

Balgownie is a classic links layout with the outward nine moving northward along the ocean, meandering in and out of the dunes, and the inward nine along a high plateau affording spectacular views of the links below and the North Sea to the left of the holes.

The first hole's tee is directly in front of the Clubhouse windows and runs downhill to a green canted to the left. Immediately behind the green is Aberdeen Beach. In most peoples' minds, the short par three, eighth is the signature hole, and depending on the wind, it will demand anywhere from a three wood to a pitching wedge. The ensuing ninth is uphill to a small green which sits adjacent to the Murcar course just north of this property. Designed by Archie and Robert Simpson in 1888, it's a beautiful seaside links which has required only lengthening by James Braid. On the inward nine, turning back to the south, the two most memorable holes are the 441 yard par four fourteenth across a dry ditch and the closing 18th, another long par four playing into the prevailing wind. We had a welcome pint or two at clubhouse after our round here.

In 2005, on a trip organized by the Vann family, we stayed at the Undy Arms Hotel just outside of Aberdeen and close to Cruden Bay and Royal Aberdeen. One of my other vices is playing the bagpipes and I have the requisite kilt and paraphernalia. My teacher advised me not to take my bagpipes; to quote her: "you don't take coal to Newcastle", so I didn't. I did, however, take the kilt with all the trimmings in a kilt carry. Checking in at the airport, the Scottish flight attendant winked and asked where my Sgian Dubh was. For the uninitiated, a Sgian Dubh is a short dagger that you wear in your right sock, just in case you get into a confrontation. I assured her that it was in my checked bag. Anyway, suffice it to say that when I wore it to dinner in Aberdeen, I was an instant hit, especially with the ladies. That's because you do not wear underwear under the kilt, only lipstick!

Murcar. Aberdeenshire, Scotland

Essentially a mirror image of Royal Aberdeen, immediately adjacent to Royal Aberdeen, sits Murcar, another good links that some raters think is better than Royal Aberdeen. I happen not to agree and do not have it listed among my favorites, because in my opinion, the redesign didn't use this land to its best advantage. It was designed by Archie Simpson in 1909 and modified later by James Braid. The outward nine runs to the south among dunes and close to the North Sea. The course turns back north on a high plateau affording great views of the course below and the the North Sea now, to the right.

Cruden Bay Golf Club, Aberdeenshire, Scotland

Until recently, the next course up the coast from Mucar was Cruden Bay, as Trump International was not finished on my last visit to the north in 2011. I hope to get back up to the Highlands and play it.

On my first trip to the Highlands in 1999, Cruden Bay was not on our itinerary, but having heard good things about this course, I insisted that we play it on the day of our arrival in Aberdeen. Looking back on my notes, it's the best 65 US dollars I ever spent for a round of golf. Let me just say that Cruden Bay is one of the three courses in The North, that if you are playing golf

in The Highlands, you should not miss. Originally
Cruden Bay was laid out by Old Tom Morris and
Archie Simpson in 1899. Later revisions to the course
were done by Tom Simpson and Herbert Fowler in
1926. It starts out bland enough with three par fours,
but the long par three fourth is a gem that highlights
the Cruden Waters and the fishing village of Port
Erroll to the left. (Figure 10)

Figure 10. The village of Port Erroll as seen from the
fourth tee at Cruden Bay

The two par fives, one on each side, are long and
hard. The fourth is the only par three on the outward
nine, but it has three par threes on the inward side,
making for an unusual card of par 36 going out and
34 coming in. Holes five, six and seven are routed
among huge sand dunes, making for great views of
the North Sea. The eighth is a drivable par four, and

the ninth crescendos upward to a high plain with spectacular views of the next four holes. (Figure 11)

Fifteen and sixteen are quirky par threes through a mountain like pass through the dunes, served up with blind shots, but in my opinion very memorable and good holes. The last two holes are somewhat anticlimactic, but overall I cannot say enough nice things about Cruden Bay and have it listed number thirty-two of my favorites. I've had the pleasure of playing it on three separate trips to Scotland and find that I like it better with each round there.

Figure 11. View from the tenth tee at Cruden Bay. Far right is the tenth green, center is the twelfth green and left is the thirteenth fairway.

The Nairn Golf Club. Nairnshire, Scotland

The next course up the coast of north eastern Scotland that I have played is Nairn. It's actually almost due west of Cruden Bay. Laid out by Archie Simpson in 1887, it was modified by Old Tom Morris and James Braid to its current routing. The first seven holes are hard by the Firth of Moray; indeed a hard slice will land you on the beach. The fifth hole requires a drive over the beach and shore, and every hole affords one a view of the Moray Firth. It's pretty flat and not very scenic unless you are there when the gorse is blooming. If it's a clear day, good views of the Highland Mountains can be seen across the Firth. We played it in 1999 just before Nairn hosted the Walker Cup, and met Matt Kuchar playing a practice round that day. We were a fairway away when he lashed a huge drive and my very vocal friend, Blake Griffith yelled: "if Kitchens swung that hard he would be in the hospital for two weeks". No truer words were ever spoken, We had a great time that day and shared stories with Kuchar and his dad after the round. I do not have it among my list of favorites however, as after the first few holes everything else is somewhat repetitive.

Castle Stuart Golf Club

If Kingsbarns is the best modern course in Scotland, Castle Stuart is just a rung below it. It is the second of the three courses that you need to play in The North of Scotland. It was designed by Gil Hanse with co-design and development by Mark Parsinen in 2009. Mr. Parsinen has developed two world class courses in the midst of other great courses in Scotland. I have it listed thirty-fifth on my list of favorites.

Castle Stuart is situated on a narrow peninsula that parallels and sticks out into the Moray Firth, just west of Nairn and six miles from Inverness. The land was granted to James Stuart, 1st Earl of Moray, by his half sister Mary, Queen of Scots, in 1561. Politics being somewhat more cruel in the sixteenth century, both he and his son-in-law were murdered and James Stuart, 3rd Earl of Moray, completed the castle in 1625. It sits at the end of the current fourth hole and is a most dramatic backdrop to the hole. (Figure 12)

Figure 12. Castle Stuart as seen from the fourth fairway at Castle Stuart GC

The first and tenth tees sit next to each other below the clubhouse making for a dramatic seascape; number one heads west and number ten heads east. The leeward side of ten is flanked by high dunes with gorse growing on them. One should remember that the first year the Scottish Open was held here in 2011, the dune slid onto the tenth fairway after a torrential rain storm occurred after the first round.

The course uses rumples (uneven bumps in the fairways and green approaches), dramatic bunkering, and infinity edges behind the green to create beautiful natural highlights to the course which is surrounded by gorse, miramar grass, and heather. Every hole has dramatic views with most of them highlighting the Moray Firth. (Figure 13). My son, Gray, and his friend

Figure 13. Castle Stuart's eleventh green, the Moray Firth behind it and the Highland peninsula in the background

Dr. Sean Hair and I spent a very memorable day here in 2011. I hope I get to come back and play the new course here now being designed by Arnold Palmer Design Group.

The Carnegie Course at Skibo Castle, Dornoch, Sutherland, Scotland

We stayed at Skibo Castle on our visit in 1999, and it was a blast. This was before Madonna and the higher prices. We arrived in Aberdeen, the wives went on up to Skibo and we guys hurried to play Cruden Bay. We made our way back around ten pm, slightly drunk after playing our game, with me navigating and Dr. Vann, not drinking, driving. My other two good friends from Wade Hampton, the late Blake Griffith and Fritz Alders, were bitching about being lost, thirsty and hungry. We took the long way over one lane dirt roads which included a riveted "cow catcher bridge". We felt we were lost so, just before arriving at Skibo, (actually we were 200 yards from the stone entrance, but didn't know it), we stopped at a phone booth for me to phone and get further directions. Fools that we were we did as instructed, drove 200 yards to arrive at the best late night supper I have ever eaten. There was everything that you could possibly want to eat on the huge table.

The saga continued on the next morning when I realized that the trip folder with The Open tickets, train tickets to Carnoustie and all the travel information were lost. Retracing my steps, I was frantically looking for the large folder in the phone booth outside Skibo's gates; it was nowhere to be found. My wife, Faye, always the inventive one, suggested we look in the large trash can adjacent to the phone booth, and there it was. Saved again from a very embarrassing moment by my lovely, patient and knowing wife!

Greg Norman was there honing his skills for The Open. He and his family could have not have been nicer, at meals and on the course. And what a course it is. Ordinarily one thinks a hotel golf course to be benign and fun. Nothing could be further from the truth at the Carnegie Club Course. It's an ecological lesson built along the Dornoch Firth, a loch, a salt water marsh and a tidal bay. The short par fours, seventh and eighth, are separated from the main body of the course by several hundred yards of lichen heath and designated as a site of Special Scientific Interest. I understand that two foursomes of unaccompanied guests are allowed on Monday through Thursday, "with the highest greens fee in Scotland".

The original course was commissioned by Andrew Carnegie in 1896 and consisted of six holes. In 1995 Donald Steel and native Tom MacKenzie designed and built the 6,625 yard par 71 course. I have it 123 on my list of favorites. I recently priced the rate per night and it calculates out as $2,400. If you stay here, definitely take a day to do the falconry outing. It's worth giving up a day of golf for this rabbit hunt.

Royal Dornoch Golf Club. Dornoch, Sutherland, Scotland

I started this chapter with the "must play" course in the East of Scotland, Muirfield, and end Part II, The North, with the "must play" course here, Royal Dornoch. I have it listed as number nine in my list of favorites. Golf was played at this site in the seventeenth century and the Club was established in 1877. The course was laid out by the legendary Old Tom Morris and designated 'Royal' in 1906. With the exception of the well-known Brora, Dornoch is the northern most course in Scotland, which accounts for the fact that tourists have been fairly scarce here.

This is a classic course hard by the Dornoch Firth. It starts out on a high plateau looking over the holes below and affording beautiful views. This is especially obvious from the third to the eighth green when the course turns back toward the clubhouse. To the left of the outward eight holes are high bluffs covered with gorse, and one can only imagine how beautiful it is when it's in full bloom. (Figure 14)

Figure 14. The eighth hole at Royal Dornoch with the bluff to the left and the ninth tee along the beach to the right

The dogleg ninth is right on the beach and the routing only turns away from the beach at the famous 14th hole named Foxy. (Figure 15) It's truly a masterpiece with elevated greens that have been imitated the world over. No one has an excuse not to come to the Highlands and play Dornoch, especially since Castle Stuart is located just south, and is planning an Arnold Palmer Design second course. Dornoch has been an inspiration to several golf course architects. The most prolific one is, of course, Donald Ross who was born in Dornoch in 1872. He immigrated to the United States in 1899 and has been responsible for designing some 413 different courses in America, including Pinehurst #2, Braeburn, Oakland Hills, Oak Hill and Seminole.

Figure 15. The fourteenth at Royal Dornoch, "Foxy", looking out at the Dornoch Firth

The other course in Dornoch is a short 6,192 yard, par 71 course, Stule. It was laid out in the early 1900's, originally designed for ladies, although many famous men pros who grew up playing here later immigrated to the US. My last piece of advice here is not to let your travel consultant talk you into playing a lesser course in The North. Play Dornoch twice!

Other courses in the North which are notable but I have not visited are:
1. Brora, the northern most course in Scotland some 15 miles north of Royal Dornoch, is a classic links course. The outward nine is on the North Sea and contains perfect examples of rumples that, in contrast to the manmade ones at Castle Stuart, are formed by God. Brora was designed by James Braid and was his favorite course. The James Braid Society is headquartered and meets here every year.
2. Durness Golf Club, founded in 1988 by local golf enthusiasts, is a nine hole tract with 18 sets of tees.

The glorious views stay the same but the challenges change enough to give the layout an eighteen hole feel. It's the most north-westerly course on mainland Britain and well worth the trip this far north.
3. Tain is south of Dornoch on the Dornoch Firth. It starts along the river Tain and moves out to the sea through high sand dunes.
4. Boat of Garten Golf Club, just off the A9 motorway south of Inverness, is a great parkland course designed by James Braid and John Stutt in 1925. If you are ahead of schedule driving back to Aberdeen or Edinburgh, it would be a good stop.
5. Moray Golf Club, east of Nairn, is also known as Lossiemouth for the town in which it lies. It was designed by Old Tom Morris in 1889 and later revised by Henry Cotton.

Part III
The West

In my opinion there is absolutely no way to do this region justice without devoting a full week of your time here. I suppose you could do East Lothian, (Edinburgh environs) and come straight west, but you would have to leave out some of the treasured courses here. I would recommend flying to Glasgow and driving south. (See sample itineraries, Page 57). All of the courses are within 60 miles and clustered along the Firth of Clyde. The major cities here are Ayr and Troon and the southern most course is Turnberry.

Trump Turnberry Resort and Golf Club, South Aryshire, Scotland

The Ailsa Course, named for the third Marquess of Ailsa on whose land the course was built, is a masterpiece. The beautiful views of the Ailsa Craig and Isle of Arran from the the high bluff where the course sits, beat Pebble Beach for ocean views. Designed and built by Willie Fernie in 1902, it wasn't really noticed until the magnificent hotel was completed in 1906. The relatively flat land surrounding the hotel and on which the course was built, was just too good a sight for the RAF to pass up. So as a consequence the site was taken over to be used as an airbase and hospital for both World Wars. From 1949 to 1951, Mackenzie Ross restored the course to its present glory; but I'm not going to describe too much of it as Trump has made major renovations which I will briefly discuss below.

The first three holes are hard par fours, followed by a beautiful par three that introduces one to the great views of the Firth of Clyde. The fourth hole's name, "Woe-Be-Tide", gives warning of the danger lurking on the left, i.e, ragged cliffs that plunge to the Firth of Clyde for the next eight holes. It's a view that's better than anything I've seen except in New Zealand. The ninth hole is Turnberry's signature hole on a high cliff next to the landmark lighthouse. When the sun is shining, it casts a shadow over the ruins of Bruce's Castle, birthplace of Robert The Bruce, Scotland's hero king.

Mackenzie & Elbert golf architects, after a careful and extensive study of the evolution and history of golf at Turnberry's Ailsa Course, have proposed major changes making even better use of the spectacular landscape and bluffs. Five holes will be extensively renovated: the sixth, ninth, tenth and eleventh all along the Firth of Clyde. Number nine will change from a par four to a long par three and will be moved much closer to the lighthouse, where an elaborate turn house will be created. Eighteen was renovated too and is now a much improved golf hole.

No discussion of this course would be complete without mentioning the four Opens held here. The first and foremost is the "Duel in the Sun", the phenomenal match between Jack Nicklaus and Tom Watson in 1977. They were tied after the first two rounds, one stroke each behind Roger Maltbie. The third round had them paired together and both shot 65 for a three shot lead over Ben Crenshaw.

Saturday's final round is considered by many golf historians as the best match in the second half of the twentieth century. Nicklaus birdied three of the first four holes, whereupon Watson birdied the next three, only to bogey the ninth and fall one back at the turn. Nicklaus birdied the twelfth to go two up, but Watson, not to be outdone, birdied the thirteenth and fifteenth. They halved the sixteenth before the real fireworks started. Watson birdied the seventeenth to go one up as Nicklaus missed a short birdie putt. Nicklaus made a brilliant recovery shot from the eighteenth rough and then made a 35 foot birdie putt forcing Watson to make a two foot putt for his birdie and a winning round of 65. (Figure 16)

At the next Open here in 1986, Greg Norman won his first of two Open titles. Nick Price won his only Open victory beating Jesper Parnevik by one stroke in 1994. After a fifteen year layoff, Watson nearly made history by tying Stewart Cink in the 2009 Open, only to lose the four hole playoff to him. A win would have given him an unprecedented sixth Open victory. Since I've devoted a page and a half to The Ailsa

Course, you can tell that I love it and have it listed as twelfth in my list of favorites. I can only hope I will return to see the renovation.

Figure 16. View of the Ailsa Course from the Turnberry Hotel with number eighteen's "Duel in the Sun" to the left

On my last trip here in 2003, with our good friends Cissy and Jay Babb, he played the Kintyre course. I had played 13 out of 14 days and was golfed out. The description of it has it rising to the brow of Bain's hill to the highest point on the course at the tenth tee. It sounds good but I was not willing to walk nine holes to find out. The Arran course is a collection of par threes and fours and I did some pitch and putt practice on my first trip here, but consider it good for a family outing or warmup to the real thing.

Jay thought The Arran was very scenic and I trust his judgment. Cissy was out and about telling the resident bagpiper that I was taking lessons and could play "Amazing Grace". The next night he called on me to play his pipes, as I didn't bring mine. Never will I make this mistake again, as his reeds were very tight and took an enormous amount of air to make a sound. By the sixth bar I was out of air and couldn't go on, very embarrassed and thoroughly tired. Thank you Cissy!

Prestwick Golf Club, South Ayrshire, Scotland

Prestwick Golf Club was formally organized in 1851 and Old Tom Morris was hired to design and build the course. He was then persuaded to stay on and become "Keeper of the Green, Ball and Club Maker". Prestwick is built on sandy land lying between the beach and the land further inland and represents the definition of a links course. Golf had been played well before 1851, but the original course crossed back and fourth over the same undulating land and was initially only 12 holes. Old Tom came back to design the remaining holes when the course was extended to 18 holes and they subsequently became the game's standard.

If St. Andrews is the home of golf, then Prestwick is the birthplace of The Open Championship. Prestwick hosted the first twelve Opens beginning in October of 1860, when in one day, eight professionals made three trips over the 12 holes for 36 holes to declare the new "Champion Golfer." Old Tom won four opens here, and his son, Young Tom Morris, won four consecutive Opens from 1868 to 1872. No competition was held in 1871, as Young Tom had retired the silver belt trophy consequently leaving nothing to play for. Prestwick stayed in The Open rota until 1925, hosting a total of twenty-four Champion-ships; for this reason alone it's worth playing.

The course has been called "kinky" and "quirky" in that it's short and has many blind shots. It is not very far from green to the next tee. The famous holes include the third, a long par five whose fairway ends at 300 yards in a vast deep bunker named the "Cardinal". The short par four fifth, "Himalayas", has a blind tee shot to a wide open fairway. The seventeenth, "Alps" has a blind tee shot over a high sand dune. The driveable sixteenth and eighteenth par fours create interesting finishes for the foursome matches usually played here. I don't have it listed in my list of favorites.

Royal Troon Golf Club, South Ayrshire, Scotland
Championship or Old Course

The Old Course is a brute and favorite of the R&A who have chosen the site eight times to host The Open Championship. It's an out and back layout, with the first seven holes running south hard by the Firth of Clyde toward Prestwick, which it adjoins. The seventh, a par four, turns slightly inland, followed by its most famous par three, "The Postage Stamp", whose tee sits high above a small green, well bunkered, and is the shortest hole in The Open rota. Another famous hole is the "Railroad" eleventh, a long, slightly dogleg left with the rail line to the right and heavy gorse to the left. In 1962 Jack Nicklaus took a ten here, hitting three balls out of bounds. The closing three holes are difficult, playing into the prevailing wind.

The Club was founded in 1878 and George Strath lengthened it when he was appointed the Club's first professional in 1881. Adam Wood was the Captain from 1893 to 1897 and donated a set of clubs with a newspaper clipping dated 1741. It's thought to be the oldest full set of clubs and originally belonged to the Stewart Kings. It just so happens that my ancestry traces me back to the clan of Stewart of Atholl, the only clan who still has an independent army. I would not miss playing this course if you are traveling to the west of Scotland and have it rated forty-two in my list of favorites.

The Portland Course, Royal Troon

This course, across the road from the Old Course, was designed by Alister MacKenzie. I only played the front nine, which comes back to the clubhouse, but I did get to play the infamous sixth hole at Portland. It seems that in 1929 Gene Sarazen had come over to play in the Ryder Cup and to qualify for The Open that year. He failed to qualify because he neglected to play a practice round here and took a double bogey on the sixth hole here.

Western Gailes Golf Club, North Aryshire, Scotland

The northern most course along the Firth of Clyde is Western Gailes. Not the best known of the courses in western Scotland, it is typical of the links courses in Aryshire. The course is situated between the sea and the railway line and both come into play, along with three burns which meander through the course. The clubhouse, with views of the Isle of Arran and Ailsa Craig, is centrally located with seven holes to the north and eleven to the south. From five to thirteen the course runs southward along the Firth and a line of dunes, then turns back northward with an out-of-bounds stone wall to the left. All the holes have great views of the Firth. I have it ranked 76th in my list of favorites and would make every effort to play it.

Machrihanish Dunes Golf Club, Argyll, Scotland

The Mull of Kintyre is a peninsula which juts out from the Scottish mainland into the Atlantic Ocean. It's a good three hour trip from Glasgow and four hours from Troon. Consequently you really have to have extra time or a strong desire to go down the two lane road to play Machrihanish Golf Club. The only other reason for going was to take a ferry to the nearby Isle of Islay and play Machrie. That all changed when David McLay Kidd finished a beautiful minimalist course, Machrihanish Dunes, in 2009. Now we have two world class golf courses within reach of a 20 minute plane ride from Glasgow or an hour and a half ferry ride from Troon, (Kintyre Express.com), both ending up in Campbeltown. Or take an auto ride as described above.

Billed as the world's most natural course, David McLay Kidd designed this course through majestic dunescapes and along the Atlantic Ocean. It is the culmination of a longstanding dream of the inhabitants of Machrihanish to build another course adjacent to the 135 year old Machrihanish Golf Club which Old Tom Morris laid out in 1876. He described the land thus: "The Almichty Maun hae had gowf in his e'e when he made this place". The routing and the positioning of its tees and greens was dictated by the lay of the land. Of the 259 acres on this site, only seven were disturbed during construction of the course. The fairways are just the land as it was encountered, only mown shorter. (Figure 17) The course measures 7,082 and may not be the longest in Scotland, but the elements, primarily wind off the Atlantic, make it a huge challenge. The course starts out toward the south for the first six holes before turning back north at the seventh tee and running hard by the raging Atlantic Ocean for the next two holes. All in all, six greens and five tees are set immediately adjacent to the beach. It gives the golfer an experience to play golf as it was meant to be played: the golfer against the elements, playing in a natural setting where grass is mowed by grazing sheep, with the links land ever changing and giving one the opportunity to craft various shots.

Figure 17. The first green at Machrihanish Dunes with the ninth fairway in the center and the Isle of Isley in the background

I decided to come here with my son once I learned of the existence of Machrihanish Dunes. It made sense to make the journey here to play not one but two great courses. We chose to fly from Glasgow round trip. I was sitting in my room at the Sunny Brae Hotel in Nairn after a 21/2 hour trip from Cruden Bay, when I saw a weather forecast for September 10, 11 and 12. It called for the remnants of Hurricane Irene, which had devastated the New Jersey Coast and caused our flight delay a week earlier, to hit western Scotland. I discussed the situation with Gray and Sean and suggested that rather than go to Glasgow, we head straight to Machrihanish Village, thereby avoiding the flight to Campbeltown the next day. I have considerable experience flying in small private planes and wasn't nervous about the flight. I knew instinctively that the flight was going to be very rough. That was definitely the case the next morning and Gray and Sean were white-knuckled the entire 30 minutes, which seemed like an hour, even to me. When we finally landed the boys were upset to say the least, as Gray said he was tired of putting his life in my hands for a trip I wanted to do. Never mind that I had warned them and given them an alternative.

I will finish this story later, but suffice it to say we played "Mach Dunes" in less than optimal conditions. The wind was blowing a sustained 45 mph, with gusts up to 55 mph. (Figure 18) Our tee time was early afternoon, but the head pro correctly stated that the longer we waited to go, the worse it would be. The caddies had not shown up so we had him phone them and set out with pull carts. We quickly learned to lay the carts down on their side as the wind would blow them over like dominoes. The first 6 holes were right into the wind and there was no way to try to keep score. After 31/2 holes, my son looked at the course map and directed me to the seventh tee, which was the start of the downwind leg, essentially on the beach.

I went over, propped my head on the tee marker and laid down. Forty minutes later when they got to the seventh tee, my black gortex rain suit was covered with sand and I looked like a snowman. The caddies showed up then and, downwind, Gray and Sean birdied the par 5 seventh and I parred it. The remainder of the round was a blur. Downwind holes we finished; upwind holes we didn't. I do not know how, but after I looked it over the next day with a buggy, I listed it sixty-five on my list of favorites.

Figure 18. The third green at Machrihanish Dunes with the seventh fairway and the Atlantic ocean in the background. Note the flag and the ocean breakers in gale force winds here.

The Machrihanish Golf Club, Argyll, Scotland

This course opened in 1876 after Old Tom Morris's visit. It's just across the street from the Ugadale Hotel which was undergoing renovation when we visited in 2011. The small town is Machrihanish Village and with the completion of "Mach Dunes", several golf cottages were completed which are ideal for a foursome traveling over to the Kintyre Peninsula. Machrihanish Golf Club's "claim to fame" is the opening tee shot across the beach and Atlantic Ocean, billed as the best opening shot in the world. (Figure 19) The course is like a "Tale of Two Cities", in that the outward nine is spectacular with holes among the dunes adjacent to The Dunes course. On a clear day the islands of Islay, Jura and Gigha are clearly visible and add to the charm of the course. Sadly the inward nine leaves much to be desired with fairways close together and bland holes. I do have it rated in my list of favorites at 120.

Figure 19. Opening hole at Machrihanish Golf Club with the beach at low tide, fairway and the remainder of the course in the background

To complete the hurricane story: the next morning before we teed off at Machrihanish Golf Club, Gray informed me that he and Sean wanted to find alternate transportation back to Glasgow. I tried in vain to find a taxi service to accommodate us. On the first hole one of the caddies said that he would take us the four hour trip for 200 pounds. The boys readily agreed to take care of it so we canceled the flight reservations. He showed up thirty minutes after our round in a Mercedes 350 coup and drove 80-100 miles per hour back to Glasgow airport in under three hours. The boys were more white-knuckled with his driving, which included passing every car in sight, than they would have been on the plane.

Others courses of note in the West:
1. Machrie Golf Club, Port Ellen, Isle of Islay, Scotland, mentioned earlier, designed by Willie Campbell in 1891 and revised by Donald Steel in 1982; reportedly it is like stepping back a century and playing. It's noted for the eighteen blind shots one takes during the round here. Because it requires another ferry ride and another day, I decided we could miss it. This year, 2017, it is being totally redesigned by David J. Russell.
2. Loch Lomond Golf Club, Luss, Scotland, designed by Tom Weiskopf and Jay Morrish in 1992, is inland and very private; consequently I have not played it. By all accounts it's great and has been highlighted as the host of several Scottish Opens.

Well, that brings us to the end of the first chapter, but I have one more story to tell regarding Scotland. Behind every great, smart and successful man is an equally great, smart and successful woman. Certainly that's true in my case, as Faye has been very supportive throughout my successful medical career and my golfing travels. She's also the most understanding woman alive!

On our eventful trip in 1992, we went over to Turnberry and I played the Ailsa Course. We had reservations to fly back from Manchester at 1:00 pm the next day. It so happened that Delta had a big flight war going with cheap tickets and despite calling at every opportunity we couldn't get through to reconfirm our tickets. This was before cell phones, travel apps and notifications regarding flights. It's a helluva long way from Turnberry to Manchester, and we were driving over 100 miles an hour on the motorway to get there. In addition to our four pieces of luggage, we had four bags of our daughter's, who was returning from spending a semester abroad. Well when we arrived at Delta check-in, they informed us that the flight departure time had been changed to 11:30 am and we had missed the flight.

I went into emergency mode, as I had patients scheduled the next day. I grabbed three ENT Journals, asked if the door had been closed, saying I would go as is, with no luggage. Well to make a long story shorter, I got on the plane, left Faye with all the luggage and she had to wait 24 hours to catch the flight the next day. I may still, after 24 years, be paying the price of that decision, but if you look in the dictionary for world's most understanding and best wife, there is a 5x7 glossy print of my wonderful, lovely, wife Faye! (Figure 20.)

Figure 20. The author and Faye, more recently on a
cruise out of Venice

Sample Itineraries

Before leaving this chapter on Scotland I will give the
reader three sample itineraries to help with trip
planning. Virtually all of my trips were taken over the
Memorial Day or the Labor Day holidays. That way
you are using one less day of vacation since most
businesses close on those Mondays. Also, less
sophisticated travelers do not see these times as
summer. Lastly, few children are out of school then
and flights are not as crowded.

The First Itinerary: If you are sure you won't get another chance to go to Scotland, I would do a more aggressive trip: eight rounds in nine days. Although, all three itineraries are aggressive.

1. Fly over to Edinburgh on Saturday. (It is harder to get on a course on Saturday.)
2. Play North Berwick or Renaissance on Sunday, the day of arrival.
3. Play the other one above on Monday or one of the courses at Archerfield.
4. Save yourself for Muirfield on Tuesday: one fourball and one foursome round.
5. Travel to St. Andrews and play Kingsbarns on Wednesday and save yourself for two rounds the next day.
6. Play the Old Course, St. Andrews either am or pm and The Castle Course that day.
7. On Friday travel to Aberdeen and play Cruden Bay, then on up to overnight at Nairn.
8. Play Castle Stuart on Saturday. It's easier to get on this relatively new course on Saturday.
9. Play Royal Dornoch on Sunday; fly from Inverness or drive back to Edinburgh.
10. Fly home on Monday and go to work Tuesday, exhausted but happy!!

The Second Itinerary: Leaving out East Lothian
1. Fly over Friday night to Edinburgh and drive up to St. Andrews Saturday morning.
2. Play the Castle or New Course that Saturday afternoon or night. It's light until midnight.
3. Play Kingsbarns on Sunday. Take in St. Andrews that evening.
4. Play The Old Course on Monday and travel to Aberdeen for a one or two night stay.
5. Play Royal Aberdeen on Tuesday.

6. Play Cruden Bay on Wednesday or double up with both these courses on Tuesday.
7. Play Trump International on Thursday and drive to Nairn or Dornoch for the evening.
8. Play Dornoch on Friday and stay there.
9. Play Castle Stuart on Saturday.
10. Travel back to Edinburgh and fly home on Sunday.

The Third Itinerary: Leaving out St. Andrews.
1. Fly to Glasgow on Friday night and drive to Prestwick or your hotel in the west.
2. Play Prestwick later that day, if possible or another course you can arrange Saturday.
3. Play Trump Turnberry Ailsa Sunday and if you have anything left, play Kintyre Course.
4. Play Royal Troon Monday or change to Sunday's suggestion. I would skip The Portland Course.
5. Play Western Gailes on Tuesday; it's on your way back toward Edinburgh.
6. Take the morning off to tour Edinburgh, go out to East Lothian and play North Berwick that afternoon.
7. Play Muirfield Thursday, fourball in the am, lunch by all means, and a foursome in the pm.
8. Play Renaissance or Archerfield Friday and/or Saturday and fly home the next day.
On Wednesday you might want to stay in Edinburgh, see the sights and take the day off. In any case, play Muirfield on Thursday and vary the other two or three courses in East Lothian and fly home Sunday.

Well, this finishes the first and major chapter of this book. I can promise more advice, more stories and analysis of many other courses to come.

Rankings of the twenty three (23) courses I have played in Scotland and their place on my list of favorites.

1. Muirfield, #6
2. Royal Dornoch Golf Club, #9
3. Trump Turnberry Alisa Course, #12
4. The Old Course St. Andrews, #16
5. Kingsbarns Golf Club, #22
6. Cruden Bay Golf & Country Club, #32
7. Castle Stuart Golf Club, #35
8. Royal Troon Golf Club Championship Course, #42
9. The Renaissance Golf Club, #59
10. Royal Aberdeen Golf Club, #61
11. Machrihanish Dunes Golf Club, #65
12. Western Gailes Golf Club, #76
13. North Berwick West Course, #87
14. Machrihanish Golf Club, #120
15. Carnegie Club at Skibo Castle Club, #123
16. Carnoustie Golf Club
17. Castle Course, St. Andrews
18. Prestwick Golf Club
19. The New Course, St. Andrews
20. Nairn Golf Club
21. The Eden Course, St. Andrews
22. Murcar Golf Club
23. Royal Troon, Portland Course

Chapter II

Ireland

Introduction

I had already been to Scotland twice for golf, when on a plane bound to Nassau in February 1993 for my home course's (Wade Hampton) winter safari, I overheard two members discussing a trip to Ireland. I had read a fair amount regarding golf in Ireland and had already decided, at the first opportunity, I wanted to go there. When Wade Hampton opened in mid April 1993, I walked up to these two individuals and asked them how their trip to Ireland had been. I was surprised by their response which was that they were actually going in three weeks. They then said that Faye and I ought to go as they had had a cancellation by one couple for medical reasons and couldn't find a replacement couple. Despite the fact that my daughter was graduating from Hollins College in mid May and my son was graduating from high school at the end of May, amazingly the dates in between worked out for us to go and we jumped at the chance. What ensued was the best trip of our lives! Trust me, that's saying a lot!

Now, as was the case when talking about Scotland, there is absolutely no way to do the Irish courses justice without taking 2-3 trips there. Again I will divide my travel advice into three areas:
1. Dublin (environs) and Northern Ireland
2. The north west-central Irish Republic
3. The south-west Irish Republic (Figure 21)

There are two "must play" courses in Northern Ireland but the courses in each of the other two areas have at least one that qualifies for that category. Most one week golf tours to Ireland start by flying to Dublin, then going north or west and flying home from Shannon. United has a direct flight to Belfast, Northern Ireland from Newark three or four times a week, so if you are spending time in Northern Ireland, I suggest you consider doing that. (See sample itineraries at the end of this chapter).

Figure 21. Map of Ireland

Part I
Dublin and Northern Ireland

Portmarnock Golf Club, Malahide, Ireland

On Christmas Eve 1893, an insurance broker, William Pickeman, and his friend George Ross rowed over to Portmarnock peninsula from Sutton, Ireland. They agreed with the owner, Mr. Jameson, to lease the southern tip of the peninsula for developing a golf course. Jameson's family had been playing golf on a rudimentary links course there since 1858. The peninsula, two miles long and situated between the Irish Sea and Badoyle Bay, was ideal links land with low sand dunes, hollows for greens and long valleys between the dunes. Thus the Portmarnock Golf Club was formed in 1894 with William Pickeman as the course's designer. The original nine holes were expanded to 18 in 1896 again by Pickeman. Subsequently in 1971 the course was lengthened to 7,500 yards and another nine holes built. I have this course rated ninety-three in my list of favorites.

The layout lies between Baldoyle Bay and the Irish Sea with the closing holes on the ocean. Number fifteen, a long beautiful par three and the sixteenth, par five, have the reputation of being as good a group of closing holes as anywhere in the world. I must admit, fresh off the plane from Atlanta, I was in awe of this course, sited on this low peninsula on the Irish Sea. It hosted the inaugural Irish Open in 1927, as well as thirteen more. The 1991 Walker Cup was also played here, reconnecting its members with many of Atlanta's Peachtree Golf Club's members and other prestigious Atlantans where the Walker Cup was held in 1989.

In 1993, when we landed in Dublin Airport, the eight men, all of whom had golf attire in our carry-on bags, left for Portmarnock and lunch. The course, located just north of Dublin, is only 15 minutes from the airport, making it the ideal venue for play on your day of arrival. One or two of the members on the trip had met and become close to Judge Ian Bamford, at that time the President of the Golfing Union of Ireland. (Equivalent to our USGA) He and other members of Portmarnock were hosting us there.

Before lunch we met Joe Carr, who prior to Darren, GMac and Rory, was Ireland's most famous golfer. We also were introduced to Sir Patrick Hillery as the past President. After this remark one of our guys, who knows as much as anyone about golf spoke up saying: "then Ian took your place". At that all of our Irish hosts laughed and informed us that Sir Hillery was the past President of the Republic of Ireland, having served in that post from 1976 to 1990, and not the past president of The Golfing Union of Ireland! It was like a foreigner in the US being introduced to Jimmy Carter and not knowing who he was.

Speaking of Jimmy Carter, I am a member of the Gridiron Secret Society, the greatest organization on The University of Georgia's campus. It's a high honor, especially for someone who did not matriculate at UGA. Everyone thinks the organization is about football as its name implies, but no, the organization has its roots in Scottish history and literature. That being said, some of the members wear kilts to the formal initiation banquet held twice a year. Indeed, I play the bagpipes at the banquet. One should remember that the traditional Scottish dress, kilt, etc., has one carrying a Sgian Dubh (a short knife) in his sock. Some ten years ago Jimmy Carter's grandson was being initiated into The Society as a student at UGA. As President Carter is a member, he gave the keynote address. I was standing next to him talking, with a deadly weapon less than three feet from his throat and the Secret Service didn't have a clue.

Back to Ireland; unfortunately I have not had the chance to play any other courses in the immediate Dublin area. I had planned a trip to Dublin and Royal County Down Golf Club when it hosted the 2007 Walker Cup Match, but had to cancel it at the last minute. I have researched many of them and will list the courses below before moving North.

1. Druids Glen Golf Club, County Wicklow. This is one of two courses 22 miles south of Dublin and is a parkland course opened in 1995. It hosted the Irish Open from 1996 to 1999. There is an inland resort here as well as a sister course, Druids Heath Course.

2. The European Club, Brittas Bay, County Wicklow. Located thirty minutes south of Dublin, this course is conceived, designed and owned by Pat Ruddy. Ruddy is one of Ireland's most prolific golf journalists, course designers and players. Its location, hard by the Irish sea, is the total package with towering dunes, salt air, wind, deep bunkers and at every turn the ocean is not only present but omnipresent. Just writing about it has convinced me to include it in my next trip to Ireland, hopefully soon.

3. The K Club, County Kildare. It hosted the Ryder Cup Matches in 2006 on a course designed by Arnold Palmer. It's located south-west of Dublin some forty miles from the city center. The other course is The Smurfit Course named for a previous owner. I tried to book a tee time when we were planning a 2007 trip,

but they wouldn't give us the time of day unless we paid $600 for a room to stay the night.

4. The Island Golf Club, Donabate, Dublin County, Ireland. Founded in 1890 and designed by Fred Hawtree and Eddie Hackett. It is located 15 miles north of Dublin's Airport on a peninsula of links land bordered by the Irish Sea, the beach of Donabate and the Browdmeadow estuary. A minimalist course, it is described as shaggy, rugged and set in low sand dunes. It was a minimalist course way before the term and courses became popular in the last decade.

Northern Ireland

Royal County Down Golf Club, Newcastle, County Down, Northern Ireland

Well, we have come to my favorite course outside the United States, Royal County Down Golf Club (RCD) ranked fourth overall, in my list. (See Favorites Courses List) We came up here on the second day of our 1993 trip and it was love at first sight for me. The gorse was in full bloom, a vivid yellow color, the grass was very green and the only other color on the course was the off-white sand. To describe it as the most beautiful sight I have ever seen on a golf course would still be an understatement. (Figure 22) I have managed to play it on each of my six trips to Ireland, with ten total rounds here. With the Mountains of Mourne as a backdrop to the south, the course stretches out along Dundrum Bay and zigzags back and forth, providing the players an opportunity to hit shots in all directions from which the constant winds blow.

Figure 22. View of the thirteenth hole
at RCD, from the high fourteenth tee, Mountains of
Mourne in the background

This championship course has had a series of
designers, beginning with Old Tom Morris who laid out
the first course which was opened in March 1889.
George Combe remodeled the Course in 1900 and
became the first green superintendent, serving until
1013. My friend Brian Coburn recently served in that
capacity and sadly died after a long illness. 1908 was
a stellar year for RCD in that Harry Vardon made
improvements to the course and King Edward VII
bestowed royal patronage upon the Club. Lastly, in
1926 Harry Colt was brought in to make further
improvements to the course.

The first three holes run parallel to the beach, the first
being a long slightly dogleg par five. The second is a
blind tee shot to a narrow fairway with the opening to
the green guarded by two bunkers, one right, one left,

five yards apart. The third is another long par four along the ocean, culminating into massive dunes that serve as a backdrop to the fourth tee. (Figure 23) After the beautiful par three fourth, there are two par fours parallel to each other, the fifth headed south back toward Newcastle, the other north into the high dunes. The short par three seventh is probably the most difficult, severest right to left slope of any hole in the British Isles, if not the world. After the eighth par four, the ninth looms as one of the most photographed holes in the world. It is played from one side of a huge mound down to a fairway sixty feet below and 260 yards from the tee. There is a ravine to the left, two bunkers in front of a raised green and the spires of the Slieve Donard Hotel in the background. This nine holes at RCD is known as being the best front nine in golf!

Figure 23. The fourth tee at RCD set among massive dunes approaching from the third green

I'm going to spare the reader a description of each hole on the inward nine. Suffice it to say that the tenth tee is adjacent to the Clubhouse and if you have been a good boy or girl, a waiter just might offer you a pint on that tee, as he did on my first trip here. The par four thirteenth, in my opinion, is the third best number thirteenth hole in the world: a dogleg right par four with a "bearded" bunker at the turn, nothing but a valley of yellow gorse and a green set in a beautiful hollow. Nothing could be better! (Figure 22)

The closing holes have been criticized, by many journalists, but I think the short par four sixteenth is a good hole and eighteen has been revised with cross bunkers to make for a dramatic finish. In summary, if you truly love golf course architecture and the beauty of nature, play this course!

As with my first exposure to Muirfield, my first day at RCD was loaded with fun and excitement. It took Danny (Dan'O) our bus driver only two days to tell that we were a fun loving group. I was in my element as none of this crowd had heard my vast repertoire of jokes, not all of which were politically correct. I spent the whole morning at the front of the bus telling stories. When we approached the border of the Republic with Northern Ireland, (keep in mind that this was in 1993 and "The Troubles" were still alive and well), Dan'O (as we had renamed him,) was worried. He advised us to be very formal and to behave as we went through a valley of concrete with cameras and guards with automatic weapons, at the checkpoint.

We sat primly and behaved through the border and arrived at the clubhouse to be greeted by Judge Bamford and other members of (RCD) with whom we had lunch and, of course, another local-liquor-after-lunch drink or two. We all had a great fourball match, dividing up, two of us and two of them. After that we showered, donned our coats and ties and had a wonderful party with them. In contrast to Muirfield, after the round is when an Irish party begins. Suffice it to say that we were overserved before we left to be on our way back to Dublin. We even polished off a fifth of Famous Grouse that I had left on the bus. When we stopped at a pub just across the border back in The Republic, several of us fell in love with two Southern Airways flight attendants and wanted to take them back to the Shelbourne Hotel with us. That was definitely the "bullet proof mentality" we were functioning under that night. In the end reason overruled our insane plans.

In 1998 I made a trip over to see Ian Bamford and Brian Coburn, who, in addition to being green superintendent at RCD for a number of years, also published the "Greenside Magazine" for greens superintendents in all of Ireland. I must attract hurricanes to the UK, as another storm, Mitch, blew in the first day I was to play with Ian and the captain of RCD. That morning the wind was blowing between 45-55 MPH. Several of the members finally decided on playing the usual Scotch Foursomes, patted me on the back and said: "let's see what Ian's friend has in him". I played but, not very well. I could manage to swing no more that a four iron. After teeing off on the eighth hole and into a gale force wind, my caddie had to literally push me forward. The balls were blowing off the green and we called it off after nine holes. I felt like I had walked at least 18+ holes that day.

A couple of other comments before we move further north. If your arrival city is Dublin and you choose to play a course north of the city, either plan to play Portmarnock, The Island Club, or County Louth/ "Baltray", named for the town where it's located; these are probably the best choices. Judge Bamford raves about Baltray, but somehow I have missed out on playing it because there has always been a conflict on my schedule. When I go back I definitely plan on playing it. Lastly, that first day, I would try and make it to Newcastle in order to stay in the Slieve Donard Hotel adjacent to RCD for two nights before moving further north. RCD has a fairly liberal guest policy: anytime Monday, Tuesday and Friday, Thursday am and Sunday pm. When you play RCD you really should change into a coat and tie and have lunch with the gentlemen members there.

There are several courses in and around Belfast, but I have always been in such a hurry to get to Royal Portrush that I have not taken the time to play or even see them.

 1. Royal Belfast: A Harry Colt design founded in 1881 and as such it is the oldest golf club in Ireland.

 2. Malone: Judge Bamford is a member and it is probably the best club in Belfast.

 3. Balmoral Golf Club: This is not connected to Queen Elizabeth II's Castle in Scotland.

 4. Belvoir Park Golf Club.

 5. Hollywood Golf Club is seven miles north of the city, with views of Belfast, County Lough and the Antrim coast. This course is most famous as the home course of Rory McIlroy.

In 1997 Sherri and Dick Vann, Faye and I combined a trip to Scotland with a trip to RCD, visiting Ian Bamford and Rosemary. We flew from Edinburgh to Belfast, having reserved a car at the airport.   Ian was to meet us as he was planning on driving us to Dublin after two days of golf, one at RCD,the other at Royal Portrush. When we landed we were all in for a shock, as our flight took us to George Best City Airport rather than Belfast International. Hertz had no large vehicles at this small airport (we were lucky they even had a rental outlet here) and we had to take a small station wagon type vehicle similar to a Subaru. We were stuffed inside this small car with all of the girls' luggage and had to tie the golf bags to the top. We looked like the scenes in "European Vacation"; but we made it to our hotel and the Dublin International Airport three days later. Moral of the story is to thoroughly check your itinerary to avoid such glitches.

Royal Portrush-Dunluce Links. Portrush, Antrim, Northern Ireland

I've played this wonderful course three times as guest of Ian Bamford, a former Captain of this great links land. It's consistently rated among the top ten in the UK, Ireland and for that matter, the world. I have it listed fourteenth in my list of favorites. Designed by Harry S. Colt and established in 1888, it is the only course to host the Open Championship (in 1951) outside of the main island of Great Britain. It has been selected to host the 2019 Open Championship.

It's located on the North Antrim Causeway Coast hard by the North Atlantic. Royal Portrush occupies three giant sandhills with views in all directions. Looking to the west one can see the hills of Inishowen in County

Donegal; out to sea is the Isle of Islay and The Southern Hebrides and, finally, to the east the Giant's
Causeway and the Skerries. The site is overlooked
by the ruins of the 13th Century Dunluce Castle,
which gives its name to the course.

The Giant's Causeway is a sight not to be missed, as
it is an area of about 40,000 interlocking, hexagonal,
basalt columns that formed as a result of an ancient
volcanic eruption. It's three miles from the town of
Bushmills and approximately seven miles from
Portrush. The tops of the columns form stepping
stones that lead from the foot of the cliffs and
disappear under the sea. Legend has it that giants
used them as stepping stones to western Scotland.

Most of the holes at Portrush are outstanding and
visually stunning, but the outward nine has the most
dramatic views of the ocean. The fourth hole is a long
par four which is 455 yards from the medal (white)
tees, with an out of bounds right and the thickest
rough I have ever had the displeasure to be in and in
and in again! The fifth hole is a 379 yard par four
dogleg to the right, back toward the ocean, named
"White Rocks". The green is very undulating, perched
on the edge of a cliff dropping to the beach, with
beautiful views of the white rocks to the east. (Figures
24 & 25)

The remainder of the outward nine and the first few
holes on the inward nine wind back and forth among
relatively flat, beautiful links land with thick heather
and gorse lining the fairways. Lastly, on the inward
nine, the fourteenth hole, named "Calamity Corner," is
a long uphill par three measuring 202 yards from the
white tees. You must hit the ball over a huge ravine to

IFigure 24. The fifth green at Royal Portrush with the
North Atlantic in the background

Figure 25. View from the fifth green at Portrush to the
cliffs, white rocks and the beach

have a chance here. The course ends with the par five seventeenth to the west, and the closing par four to the east, back to the clubhouse. I have no interesting stories to relate here, but if at all possible, tour the Bushmills Distillery, sample the Irish whiskey, and by all means stay at the Bushmills Inn.

Royal Portrush Valley Links, Portrush, Antrim, Northern Ireland

As the name suggests, this course lies in a valley between huge sand dunes and the Dunluce Links, which sits on higher ground. I probably should, but have not taken the time to play it.

Portstewart Golf Club, Strand Course, County Londonderry, Northern Ireland

Just west of Portrush, this is another well-known golf club which consists of a fifty-four hole complex. The championship, Strand Course is the only one we will discuss. The Club was founded in 1894 with the redesign done by Willie Park, Jr. in the 1920's. Not until the late 1980's was a redesign effected. Local architect, Des Giffin updated the course; using land close to the North Atlantic he added seven new holes. The opening two holes are spectacular, with the first hole on a high dune with a 360 degree view, and the ocean on the right. The second, after cutting through high dunes, ends in a vale cut into the dunes. The next five new holes consist of two par threes and two par fives, interspaced with a par four: they are good! After that the course is bland without much else to recommend it. I do not have it in my list of favorites.

*Castlerock Golf Club, County Londonderry,
Northern Ireland*

Located a few miles further west of Portstewart and just north of Coleraine, Castlerock is a classic links course. It was founded in 1901, updated by Ben Sayers in 1908 and further refined by Harry Colt in the early 1930's. The signature fourth hole, a par three named Leg O' Mutton, requires a tee shot over a burn to a smallish green. Other than being a great example of a links course, I was otherwise unimpressed with this course and do not have it rated.

Accompanying me in 1998, to Northern Ireland, was Dr. Vann, Steve Warren and the late Blake Griffith, the latter two, members of Wade Hampton. It turned out that a man in business class had fallen and cut the skin above his eyebrow on our flight over to Dublin. Since I am a facial plastic surgeon, I ended up repairing the laceration, saving him at least a half day on his vacation. As we were getting off the plane one of the stewardess said that Delta couldn't pay me but the crew wanted me to have several bottles of wine and champagne. Well, during the next two nights we all made short work of the wine.

After we finished playing Castlerock we headed back to Dublin. At the border, which was much more relaxed in 1998 than in 1993, we stopped for gas. Someone suggested we get some orange juice and drink mimosas back to Dublin. When Blake opened the bottle there was a very loud bang; whereupon we looked around to see that a local Irishman had literally climbed up on top of the gas pump to avoid a blast! This was not real smart, but just shows you that violence is still on everyone's mind. But to reassure you, I have never felt in danger being in Northern Ireland.

Part II
The North-West Irish Republic

Ballyliffin Golf Club, Inishowen County, Donegal, Ireland

At Magilligan, Northern Ireland one crosses the Lough Foyle by ferry to Greencastle in the Republic of Ireland. It's a relatively short ride north west to Ballyliffin. I had resisted the urge to come this far north until several of my friends from Montgomery, AL, highly recommended I go. It is the northern most golf club in Ireland and worth the effort if you are traveling to Portrush. The club consists of two outstanding, contrasting, links courses with panoramic views of the countryside, coastland and ocean. The Club was founded in 1947, but it took until 1973 for the first eighteen holes to be completed to form the Old Course.

Ballyliffin Golf Club Old Links

This course, recently updated by Sir Nick Faldo, is primarily inland until the the thirteenth hole. From there to the seventeenth tee it's located hard by the Atlantic Ocean with good views. I would recommend playing the back nine after a round on the Glashedy Links, but do not have it listed in my list of favorites.

Ballyliffin Golf Club, Glashedy Links

This is a true championship links designed by Pat Ruddy and Tom Craddock. It sits on one of the finest piece of links golfing terrain in Ireland, and that's saying a lot. Opened in August 1995, it's worth the trip up here to play it. The back nine is closer to the ocean and traverses some great dunes. From the tenth to the seventeenth, the ocean is in constant view, with ten and eleven on a plateau above the sixteenth and seventeenth. The other prominent structure is the Glashedy Rock which, off the coast, is a prominent feature of the ocean views. The outward nine twists and turns among high dunes strewn with rocks and boulders. (Figure 26) In 2006 my foursome included Drs. Ned Turnbull, Frank Kelly and Charlie Hubbard; all played better than I did on

Figure 26. Glashedy Links number nine is in the foreground with the first tee to the left and the eighteenth green in front of a modest clubhouse. The town of Ballyliffin is in the background.

this demanding tract of 6,464 yards, prompting me to move up to the red tees for the remainder of the trip. I have it rated 103rd in my list of favorites because of the scenery here.

Just west of Ballyliffin on another peninsula is Rosapenna. It requires a long drive back south from Ballyliffin and then up north to this venue so, because there is no connecting ferry, I have chosen not to make this trip. It has two courses, The Old Tom Morris Links and another championship links, "Sandy Hills", designed by Pat Ruddy.

Donegal Golf Club, Murvagh, Republic of Ireland

A relatively new course, founded in 1959, Donegal Golf Club moved to wonderful links land, the Murvagh Peninsula in the early 1970's. Revisions have been performed by Pat Ruddy. The course is bordered by the Atlantic Ocean on one side and Donegal Bay on the other. It has panoramic views of the Bluestock Mountains to the north. It's a 7,300 yard par 73, with three demanding par fives on the front side and two on the back.

All in all I wasn't that impressed with the layout, although it does resembles Muirfield, with the outward nine taking an outer loop clockwise and the inward nine taking an inner loop counterclockwise. (Figure 27) I do not have Donegal listed in my list of favorites, but there is a small story illustrating my driving skills or lack thereof. The aforementioned three orthopedic surgeons hadn't had enough golf after eighteen and wanted to play an emergency nine.

I chose to drive back to the hotel and take a nap. The left mirror on our Land Rover was a casualty 200 yards past the parking lot as I hit a directional sign on my way out, very similar to my driving at Edinburgh.

Figure 27. The front nine at Donegal Golf Club with the Bluestock Mountains in the background

County Sligo Golf Club, Rosses Point, County Sligo, Ireland

The next good golf course south of Donagal is County Sligo Golf Club. By my second trip over to Northern Ireland, Judge Bamford, realizing how much I loved links golf, insisted that I travel to this venue, commonly known as Rosses Point for the peninsula on which the course sits. It's almost directly due west, across Ireland from Newcastle. In 2002 my son Gray, my close friend R.W. (Butch) Nicholson and his father, Nick, went over. Gray was too young to drive and Nick too old so they sat in the back of our rented van and let Butch and I drive while they drank scotch and smoked cigars. Never too young or old for that!

The course, located in picturesque Rosses Point, commonly referred to as simply "The Point", was founded in 1894 as a nine hole course. The Club now has twenty-seven holes: The Championship eighteen and the nine hole Bomore Course. The West of Ireland Championship has been played here every Easter since 1923. The original clubhouse was designed by a noted Dublin architect in 1912, with the Tudor style facade facing the practice putting green.

The Point was updated and extended to eighteen holes in 1927 by Harry S. Colt. The twelfth hole, a par five, tumbles downhill to the Atlantic Ocean and from the twelfth to the eighteenth the holes lie next to three beaches separated from each other by two small brooks. The first hole is an uphill par four and the second another short par four that measures 320 yards, severely uphill, making the tee shot difficult to judge. The wind is always blowing off the ocean, but after the opening two holes, number three and five are significantly downhill par fours.

The tenth and eleventh are not on the ocean, they are closer to the Benbulben Mountain which dominates the landscape as a dramatic, flat, mesa type of land mass. (Figure 28) The fourteenth, a 355 yard par four that, with the prevailing wind often plays like a par five, is known to be Tom Watson's favorite hole here. The seventeenth is the best of the finishing holes, a long par four requiring a long second shot to an amphitheater green. I have this course listed sixty-seventh in my list of favorites.

Figure 28. Benbulben Mountain dominating the
eastern landscape at Rosses Point

Ian Bamford and several of his Irish friends accompanied us when we played here in 2002, so the Club
basically ran out of caddies that day and I had to take
a boy, Ben, who couldn't have been over twelve and
not five feet tall. When we finished, Nick asked Ian
how our caddies were, whereupon he said all of them
were acceptable, for their age, especially Wee Ben,
that's what we had nicknamed him. Later, Wee Ben
had a nice looking teenage girl in the restaurant
buying her lunch with his earnings, which makes
makes me wonder if Wee was an appropriate name
for him.

Enniscrone Golf Club, Enniscrone, County Sligo, Ireland

The Dunes or Championship course was designed by Eddie Hackett in 1970 and construction was finished in 1972. He designed several holes through the dunes but left most of the dunes relatively undisturbed. A new clubhouse was built in 1989 and by 1999 the potential of Enniscrone becoming a world class course was realized when Donald Steel was commissioned to reroute the course directly into the dunes. The result was six new holes directly into and on the very high dunes along the Moy Estuary. The six holes of the original course on flatter ground were converted to a nine hole course by adding three new ones and is called Scurmore for the area's beach.

The course routing is clever with the first two holes in the dunes off the Atlantic Ocean behind the closing holes hard by the ocean. The next six holes rotate in a counter-clockwise direction slightly inland. Beginning at the ninth the holes occupy high dunes above the Moy Estuary, with the tenth offering marvelous views of the estuary. The eleventh is an uphill par three, and the twelfth an unusual short par four with the green cut out onto a massive shelf at the bottom of a giant dune. (Figure 29) The thirteenth has a long drop from an elevated tee back to the flatter part of the course. The closing four holes are hard by the Atlantic with spectacular views of the ocean, with the eighteenth on flatter ground returning to the clubhouse. I have Enniscrone rated seventy-one in my list of favorites. (Figure 30)

Figure 29. The twelfth hole at Enniscrone, cut from
the center of a massive dune

Figure 30. The author on the eleventh tee at
Enniscrone, looking back at the tenth green and the
Moy Estuary in the background

Carne Golf Links, Belmullet, County Mayo, Ireland

This course, in my opinion, is the only "Must Play" course in the North West area of Ireland. I came here with my son Gray, Butch and Nick Nicholson in 2002 and was very impressed with the size and shape of the dunes, the overall layout and the ocean scenery. We played in a moderate to heavy rain; the only saving grace was that Nick and I had an enclosed buggy. On the elevated seventeenth tee, after it had cleared a bit I took out my camera and asked Gray to take a picture. He asked me what of? I turned to him and said: "Point the camera 360 degrees around this tee; every view will be picture perfect." (Figure 31)

Figure 31. The seventeenth fairway at Carne from the tee on the highest sand dune I have ever seen

The course is located in Belmullett, close to the end of the earth. The next land mass west is Nova Scotia. You drive for approximately two hours over gradually narrowing roads until you get to the town, with Carne

Golf Links two miles further on the peninsula. As an old Highlands, NC mountain man who taught me how to fly fish years ago said: "You have to step on several cow patties to get to the cream and butter". This course, designed by the legendary Eddie Hackett in 1992-93, was the last course he completed and has become one of the premier links courses in Ireland and is a true gem in Mayo County.

The course starts out with a dogleg par four with a large dune at the dogleg covered with ivory colored burnet roses in the summer. The second is a short par three with a deep bunker at the front right of the green. The third is a sweeping par four with an undulating fairway, with the whole expanse of the hole laid out from the tee. Everywhere one looks there are massive dunes, the highest and most elegant I have ever seen. (Figure 32).

Figure 32. The majestic dunes at Carne Golf Links

The outward nine returns to the clubhouse with the short par five tenth "Echo" next. The front of the green is guarded by two bunkers and sheltered by huge dunes which can give confusing sounds or echoes on approach. The thirteenth, the second of three par threes on the inward nine, brings one out to the sea and the furthest point from the clubhouse. The eighteenth, a par five, gives one breathtaking views of Blaksod Bay. I have it listed at twenty-seven in my list of favorites. It's that good!

There is a new nine holes here, Kilmore, that if it is more spectacular than the original eighteen, I need to see it. The design work was shared by Jim Engh and Ally Macintosh. Tom Doak says that "three or four of these holes go straight to the top of the class."

Again, I hesitate to recommend lodging or hotels, but in the northwest region there is no better spot for my money than the twelve room Saint Ernans House located on a small island two miles south of Donegal. It's quaint and off the beaten path.

Part III
The South-West Irish Republic

Since I mentioned lodging, there are two wonderful inns in the southern part of western Ireland. The closest one to Lahinch and Ballybunion is Adare Manor. It is a restored Neo-Gothic Manor just south of Limerick. When we were there in 1993 the un-completed golf course had been graded but not completed, but the accommodations in the Manor House were great. Since then the RTJ, Sr. design has undergone an extensive renovation in 2016 by Tom Fazio.

The second Inn is Sheen Falls Lodge on the Sheen River just south of Kenmare. It's close to the Ring Of Kerry, Waterville and Tralee. It's the best small hotel I have ever stayed in. At least one of these is a must stay and definitely a must stay if your wife is with you.

Lahinch Golf Club, County Clare, Ireland

The idea of a golf course in this part of western Ireland was hatched by officers of the Black Watch Scottish Regiment of the British Army. They all were fierce and dreaded fighters, so much so that Germans hated the sound of bagpipes after World Wars I and II. In 1894, Old Tom Morris was invited to design and construct a course. He said Lahinch was the finest natural course he had ever seen and preceded to put most of his time and effort routing the holes through the sandhills adjacent to the Liscannor Bay. Lahinch was not recognized as a great course until after 1926 when Alister MacKenzie rerouted all of the holes across Liscannor Road, incorporating huge sand dunes, the shore of Liscannor Bay and the banks of the river, into a magnificent eighteen holes.

Lahinch has hosted the South of Ireland Champion-ship since 1893, and John Burke has won it eleven times. In 1935 the Golf Committee decided that the undulating greens that MacKenzie had designed were too tough and had Burke flatten them out. Fortunately the long, narrow ninth and the small eleventh survived and in 1999 Martin Hawtree reinstated the charact-eristics of the original MacKenzie designed greens.

The first two holes run roughly parallel to the town, separated by Liscannor Road. The third is a 446 yard par four. The drive, even from an elevated tee, is blind into a hidden fairway. The hole requires a very long approach to an elevated green sitting on the shore of Liscannor Bay. The fourth tee is on the beach; the shot must find a narrow fairway and the second shot must negotiate the "Klondyke", a huge sand dune in the middle of the fairway. This bizarre hole, typical of Old Tom Morris, is followed by another strange hole, "The Dell". It's a blind par three to a green tucked into the bottom of surrounding sand dunes. One must follow a white stone to line up this shot and hope the tee shot clears the protecting dune and finds the green. The sixth, like the third, runs back to Liscannor Bay with beautiful views of it. The seventh runs along a high plateau above the water and is probably the most scenic hole. The eighth and ninth holes turn back inland, the former an uphill par three and the latter a demanding par four with a large drop off to the left side of the green.

The tenth and eleventh are essentially new Hawtree holes with MacKenzie greens. The twelfth, a par five parallels the Inagh River. On our trip here in 1993 one of our long hitting Wade Hampton players nearly got into a fight with his caddie who assured him he couldn't drive the green on the short par four thirteenth. Not only did he drive it, Buddy Rice hit the ball so far over into a deep ravine that it was totally unfindable. The sixteenth is a downhill par three beside the river, and the last two holes are uphill, protected by MacKenzie bunkers. I think Lahinch is the "Must Play" course in the southwest and have it ranked thirty-ninth in my list of favorites.

Trump International Golf Club-Doonbeg, County Clare, Ireland

Some thirty miles south of Lahinch on a stretch of high dunes and a beautiful beach is the new development of Doonbeg. Unfortunately the tree huggers got to it before Greg Norman and, for the sake of a tiny snail, prevented development of the best links land for golf short of Carne. The course opened in 2002 and shortly thereafter I played it with my son and the Nicholsons. Recently purchased by Donald Trump, it's now known as Trump International Golf Club and Hotel, Ireland.

The course routing is a single loop of nine holes out and nine holes back. Because of the constraints of the environmentalists, several holes cross over one another much less elegantly than on The Old Course. This "natural routing" within the dunes that Norman was allowed to build on, results in the uncommon combination of five par five holes and five par three holes. The ocean is allegedly visible from sixteen of the eighteen holes, but some of them might require a periscope. On the other hand The Lodge, consisting of 218 rooms or suites, is reported to be elegant and a great place to stay. It was not finished when we visited. You have already guessed that I do not have it listed in my list of favorites.

Ballybunion Golf Club (Old Course), County Kerry, Ireland

Probably the most famous course in The Irish Republic or Northern Ireland is located south of Lahinch and Doonbeg and slightly north of the Ring of Kerry. The Club was organized in 1893 when twelve greens were laid out upon the links and dunes with the idea that another six holes could be completed later. Similar to Lahinch, The Black Watch Regiment and The Prince of Wales Regiment (Royal Canadians) had a hand in initial and later development. Several other men and well known architects of their day contributed to further design. Those included: Captain Lionel Lloyd Henderson in 1906, Tom Simpson in 1926, when the course was extended to eighteen holes, and finally Tom Watson in 2000, when he redesigned the fifth tee, the seventh green and added fourteen bunkers.

Tom Watson fell in love with Ballybunion after his initial visit in 1981 and has returned many times both before and after his redesign work. I have played the Old Course here two times, the first in 1993 (when it beat me to death) and again in 2002 at the insistence of Nick Nicholson. That year we had stayed north of Ballybunion and had to catch a ferry over the wide Shannon River to make our tee time. We just made the ferry in the last group, were delayed getting off and had only two minutes to make our tee time. I'm hyperactive on a good day and with all the rushing around I was a basket case on the first tee. I shanked my first tee ball into the cemetery just right of the first tee, took a mulligan, which was booed, and shanked another barely in play on the right. So a double bogey on the first.

The second is a long par four that has a green high up in the dunes. The sixth hole is magnificent, sweeping down to a green perched on a cliff above the Atlantic Ocean. I think the scenery calmed me, my jitters were over as I played the seventh the most scenic in that it is along the bluff overlooking the ocean for its entire length. The eighth and ninth go back inland, while the tenth tumbles back down to the cliffs overlooking the ocean. The eleventh, like the seventh is along the Atlantic, with the fifteenth, sixteenth and seventeenth giving more spectacular vistas from the bluffs down to the ocean. Having said all of this, I guess it's the "Must Play" course for the low handicapper in the southwest region. Like Carnoustie, however, it beat me up from one to eighteen, consequently I have it listed at seventy-third in my list of favorites.

The Cashen Course at Ballybunion

This is a relatively new course designed by Robert Trent Jones, Sr. in the high dunes just south of The Old Course. When we first visited Ballybunion, four of our eight traveling wives played it and thought it was awful, narrow with small greens. I haven't played it and won't say anything else about it.

Tralee Golf Club, West Barrow, Ardfert, County Kerry, Ireland

The Club was formally organized in 1896 with several sites for nine hole courses until the Club acquired a parcel of land located on a peninsula at Barrow, next to the Atlantic Ocean. The course opens up with two holes which have spectacular views of the beach, behind the first and all the way down the right side of the second. Located behind the third green are the ruins of a tower that dates back to 1190. The Academy Award winning film "Ryan's Daughter" starring Robert Mitchum and Sarah Miles was filmed on this beach.

Designed by The Arnold Palmer Group, the outward nine sits on a peninsula with relatively flat dunes and returns to the clubhouse. However, the inward nine lies adjacent to the beach in high dunes, hard by the ocean. The massive uphill par five fourteenth hole cured me from smoking cigars on the golf course. In 1993, while playing Tralee, my friend Angus Hughes offered me a massive cigar on the eleventh green. He smokes at least two cigars during a round of golf. Halfway up the fairway my young caddie couldn't go any further and I had to help him pull the trolly up that steep hill. On the green I was too winded and dizzy to putt. To this day, even riding in a cart, I have never touched a cigar until the nineteenth hole.

The views are good here and Tralee may be the exception to Judge Bamford's rule stating why play an American course when you've traveled to Ireland. I don't have this course in my list of favorites.

Waterville Golf Links, County Kerry, Ireland

The next great golf venue south west of Tralee is Waterville. Due west of Tralee is the Dingle Peninsula and the peninsula south of this is the area in Ireland known as Kerry, made famous with the oval road, the "Ring of Kerry". The furthest point west on this road is Waterville Golf Links situated in the southern shore of Ballinskelligs Bay. The Club's origins are due to the hundreds of workers and technicians who settled here in the 1880's associated with the trans-atlantic cable, switching stations, and communications between Europe and the United States. The Club was formally organized when it joined with the Waterville Athletic Club in 1889. Other than the fame acquired when

Charles A. Lindberg first made landfall at Waterville on his historic first transatlantic flight in 1927, it lay dormant until it was acquired by John A. Mulcahy in 1960. Eddie Hackett, the famous Irish architect, came in to reconfigure the flat front nine and design the second nine into more rugged exposed dunes and links land.

We were there in May of 1993, some five years after another group of Irish Americans bought the Club and set about carrying on the tradition of this wonderful links. Together with the course, they acquired the four-star Waterville House, its fishery and Butlers Pool, to bring some of the best fishing in the world to Waterville. My friend, Tom Fazio, did a major renovation, which included ongoing coastal management that has transformed this wonderful links to a model of environmental preservation. I asked him recently to comment on his renovation of Waterville: "Waterville was a labor of love. The setting is second to none and we were fortunate to be able to contribute over a number of years to a gradual improvement process that allowed the golf course to have a unified visual and strategic presence. It was my first course in Europe and is a place I enjoy visiting year after year."

The course starts out on flat land that moves to the shore of Ballinskelligs Bay by the third hole, hugs the Bay for two more holes before turning itself back inland. The tees become gradually more elevated as the routing moves between the dunes. Gary Player's favorite hole, the par five eleventh, runs forever through magnificent dunes. "You feel almost in a world of your own as you stroll along the fairway", he said. Beginning at the fifteenth green, the closing holes are adjacent to the beach all the way to the eighteenth. The seventeenth, "Mulcahy's Peak", is the highest point on the property and probably would be the signature hole among several others on this beautiful Bay. After my one visit here in 1993, before Tom Fazio worked his magic, I had this course ranked ninety-five. After my research on this course I would rate it higher based on Mr. Fazio's comments. Indeed, many raters feel that if the location were not so remote, it would have given Royal Portrush a run for its money hosting the 2019 Open.

Old Head Golf Links, County Cork, Ireland

Once I saw the photographs of Old Head, I was sold on seeing it in person. This site is an amazing, diamond shaped peninsula jutting out two miles into the Atlantic Ocean on the southern tip of Ireland. The people who had a hand in the developing, designing and construction of it, read like a who's who in Irish golf. The brainchild of John and Patrick O'Connor, Ron Kirby, former designer with Nicklaus Golf, Paddy Merrigan, Australian golf designer, Liam Higgins and Eddie Hackett, former Irish pros and Dr. Joe Carr, Ireland's premiere amateur, all had input. The course, measuring over 7,200 yards, comprises five par fives, five par threes and eight par fours. Nine holes play along dizzying cliff tops with all eighteen holes providing unbelievable ocean views. With six sets of tees, the course is playable by all levels of golfers.

When we arrived in early October 2000, my close friend and member of our foursome was absent. It seems that despite being an amateur pilot and plane owner, the late Blake Griffith was deathly afraid of heights. He took one look at the brochure and views of Old Head and immediately had an emergency in one of his upstate South Carolina textile plants and instead of flying to Cork, flew back to Atlanta. The day we arrived the wind was blowing 25 MPH with a steady rain. We played the front and skipped eleven through fourteen, but finished the dramatic eighteenth on the high dune just to the right of the lighthouse. The weather was much better the following day, except for the wind. All three of us played worse with the improved weather. I think you concentrate better when you have adverse conditions to make you focus.

It's worth the effort to come here even it you do nothing but walk around the lovely town of Kinsale, eat, drink and be merry. I will go on record as saying that this is the best small village I've ever visited. It is a sophisticated seaside town set between the hills and the shore, with small medieval streets and historical links to French, Spanish, British and American interests. The food is wonderful and the accommodations range from small B&B's to 4 and 5 star hotels and mansions. I cannot say enough nice things about Kinsale.

Before leaving the southwest of Ireland, I want to mention the Killarney Park Hotel. Set in the middle of Killarney's City Center and adjacent to the famous Lake Leane, it's a site to see and a good place to have a leisurely lunch, as we did in 1993. The Killarney Golf and Fishing Club offers three inland, parkland courses with large views of the Lake: they are Killeen, Mahony's Point and Lackabane.

Lastly, there is the Cork Golf Club founded in 1888 and significantly redesigned by Alister MacKenzie in 1927. Do not do what I did in 2000 and skip this course. Located at Little Island close to Cork City Center, the routing is unique, running through old limestone quarries and the inner reaches of the Cork Harbor. One better believe that if I had known MacKenzie had redesigned this course in the 1920's, I would not have missed it.

I would be letting you down if I didn't recount what all members of our touring group in 1993 considered my best shot of the trip. The last night of our trip we ate in a wonderful restaurant in Kenmare and as usual the wine was flowing. Someone decided that we needed to hit some final balls down the main drag in the small town. So my four iron shot was hit straight, square down the center of the street and rolled 300+ yards without hitting anything, not even one side mirror was damaged!

As I did after Chapter I, I will give the reader three sample itineraries that I would recommend in planning a trip to Ireland.

Itinerary 1. "The Best and Nothing but the Best"
All courses in this list are on my list of favorites.
 1. Fly to Dublin, Ireland, Saturday or a Sunday night.
 2. Play Portmarnock the day of arrival and go on to Newcastle. Overnight at The Slieve Donard Hotel.
 3. Play Royal County Down on a Monday or Tuesday, come in, change into a jacket and tie and eat lunch. If possible go back out for a "Scotch" Foursome (alternate shot). You cannot play RCD as a guest on Wednesday or Saturday.

4. Travel to the Antrim coast and stay at Bushmills Inn; or you could spend another night in Newcastle.

5. Play Royal Portrush Dunluce Links. If your group is aggressive, stay and play the Valley course at Portrush, spend the night at Bushmills Inn and get an early start to Rosses Point or County Sligo Golf Club.

6. Play Rosses Point late Wednesday,   Since it has been nine years since I have been in the west I hesitate to recommend lodging.

7. Play Enniscrone Golf Club on Thursday.

8. Play Carne Golf Club on Friday.

9. Play Lahinch Golf Club on Saturday.

10. Fly home Sunday morning out of Shannon International Airport.

That's seven top courses in eight days.

Itinerary 2. The East of Ireland.

1. Fly to Belfast on Saturday, US Airways has direct flights from Newark, but not daily.

2. Play in Belfast after arrival on Sunday: Royal Belfast, Malone or McIlroy's Hollywood.

3. Travel to the Antrim Coast and overnight in Bushmills Inn.

4. Play Royal Portrush, on Monday.

5. Travel south to Newcastle and overnight at The Slieve Donard Hotel.

6. Tuesday, play Royal County Down; dress and have lunch then play a 'Scotch" Foursome and overnight in Newcastle; you cannot go wrong there.

7. On Wednesday travel the short distance to County Lough or as it's called, Baltray Golf Club. Play here on the way south to Dublin.

8. Play Portmarnock Golf Club on Thursday, spend Wednesday and Thursday nights in Dublin.

9. Travel south 30 miles and play The European Club on Friday.

10. Stay south of Dublin and play Druids Glenn
Saturday.
11. Come back to Dublin International and overnight
before flying out the next morning.
Again, that's seven courses in eight days.

Itinerary 3. The South West of Ireland.
 1. Fly to Shannon on Saturday evening.
 2. After arrival Sunday, play Lahinch.
 3. Head north and overnight somewhere between
Lahinch and Rosses Point.
 4. Play Rosses Point or County Sligo Golf Club on
Monday.
 5. Travel south to Bellmullet and play Carne on
Tuesday.
 6. Cross the Shannon River Estuary by ferry and play
Ballybunion on Wednesday.
 7. Go further south along The Ring of Kerry and play
Waterville on Thursday.
 8. Overnight in Kinsale and play Old Head on Friday.
 9. Come back north and play Tralee on Saturday or if
you are golfed out stay in Kinsale another night.
10. Overnight at Shannon Airport for the flight home
on Sunday.
All three of these suggested itineraries are
aggressive, playing seven out of eight days, but all
are flexible, allowing cancellation for sightseeing. In
general the last suggested course in each group is
the one I would skip.

List of the seventeen courses I have played in
Northern Ireland and The Republic of
Ireland and their ranking on my list of favorites.

1. Royal County Down Golf Club, #4
2. Royal Portrush Golf Club, Dunluce Links, #14
3, Carne Golf Club, #27
4. Lahinch Golf Club, #39
5. Rosses Point, County Sligo Golf Club, #67
6. Enniscrone Golf Club, #71
7. Balleybunion Golf Club, Old Course, #73
8. Portmonarck Golf Club, #93
9. Waterville Golf Club, #95
10. Ballyliffin Golf Club, Glashey Links, #103
11. Portstewart Golf Club
12. Donegal Golf Club
13. Tralee Golf Club
14. Old Head Golf Links
15. Trump International Golf Club-Doonbeg
16. Castlerock Golf Club
17. Ballyliffin Golf Club, Old Course

Chapter III

England

I have not tried to circumnavigate England, playing all areas as I have in Scotland and Ireland, simply because, while there are good courses scattered throughout all areas, there are only two or three that offer a variety of courses in one area. Examples are

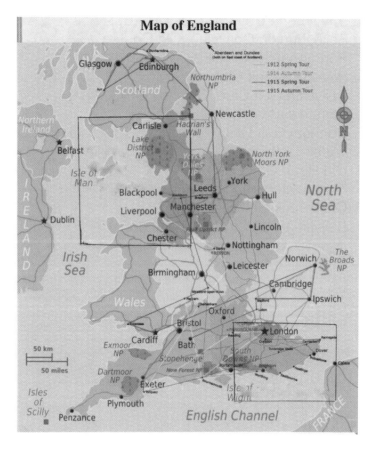

Figure 33. Map of England with the two best areas for golf in boxes

Ganton and Alwoodley in the north-east, Cavendish and Kingston in the Midlands, Royal West Norfolk and Woodhall Spa in East Anglia and St. Enodoc and Royal North Devon Westward 'Ho!' in the south-west. Remember to put the exclamation point behind Ho so as not to offend an Englishman, unless you mean to.

That being said, there are two areas in England that are not to be missed if you are a true traveling golfer, especially to the United Kingdom. The first is the area south of London. If you are married or have a significant other, they will never turn down a trip to London, especially King's Street for antiques or high fashion in Knightsbridge. So first I will discuss this area where you can often take the train down and play golf while your love is shopping. Then I'll look at north-west England, location of three venues on The Open rota and home to several other world class links courses. (Figure 33)

Part I
South of London and Surrey

Park Palace Golf Club (Hampton Course), Berkshire, England

In 1992, after three days of the more sophisticated sightseeing venues while visiting my daughter in London, I walked out of our hotel, with my golf clubs, got in a cab and asked him where the closest golf club was and what was the fare. When he said 30 pounds I said go for it. Where we ended up was at this golf course adjacent to Hampton Court, Castle of Henry VIII, right up my alley as a British history buff. I had brought 6-8 Augusta National divot tools and had also grabbed a handful of ball markers on my last visit there and started passing these out to the pro, staff in the shop and my assigned playing companions. You would have thought they were made of solid gold. To say the least, I was well received and had a wonderful experience with the members of my foursome.

The course is located on the grounds of Home Park that represented the King's recreation and hunting grounds. The area is also referred to as Bushy Park, adjacent to the walls of Hampton Court. The course is a contrast of sandy inland links-like land and a typical parkland course. Wildflowers and flowering grasses line most fairways, and when I was there in May it was stunning. On about the third hole I asked one of my playing companions what grass the course consisted of; his response was priceless. In that inimitably upper crust accent, he said: "Just grass". Maybe more of us should take this attitude and worry less about the stimpmeter.

My next visit to southern England took place in 1997 when the group of Wade Hampton couples numbering eight, and now carrying the name of The Rendezvous on our blue blazers, descended on Pennyhill Park Hotel in the Surrey area of England. Located between Ascot (for racing), Sunningdale and Wentworth, it is a wonderful place to relax and explore the golfing options of the south London area which are plentiful. It also has a short chipping course which is great for getting familiar with the conditions there.

Foxhills Golf Club Longcross Course, Berkshire, England

The golfers, eight men and four women had arrived basically all together and it took William McKee, the late founder of Wade Hampton, less that an hour to organize an unscheduled round on this resort course. The course is narrow, lined with beautiful Scotch pine, beech and silver birch trees. The outgoing nine returns to the clubhouse, but even after our trans-atlantic flight, not one of us quit at the turn. As I recall, it had more cross burns and burns lining the fairway than any other course I've played in the United Kingdom. The Resort and adjoining hotel have two other courses: the older Bernard Hunt course and the par three Manor course.

Sunningdale Golf Club, The Old Course, Berkshire, England

Founded in 1900, The Old Course was designed by Willie Park, Jr. and opened for play in 1901. Almost immediately Harry Colt adopted this course as his home and became its first Secretary. Later as Captain, he redesigned The Old, giving it a more intimate feel. In 1923 he designed the second course here, The New. Of course he went on to design over 100 courses in the UK and America including Swinley Forest in Surrey. He is also reported to have been very influential with George Cobb in the development of Pine Valley. It was originally thought that turf grasses would not grow inland but "The Old" was very successful, disproving that premise. I'm going to dwell on the Old Course as this was the venue that we played. I consider it the "must play"course in this area of England.

The original course was set in a heathland area with wonderful sandy soil. The fairways are lined with a mixture of pine, birch and oak trees. The signature tree is a stately oak just off the eighteenth green and as such is the Club's logo. Many regard Sunningdale as the ideal place to play golf, as the heathland turf is probably the finest in the world. Its location, thirty miles south-southwest of London, offers the golfer an opportunity to come down for a day or a week.

The most stunning and remarkable holes were first the fifth: from an elevated tee the hole is clearly defined and bordered by heather, golden grass and the dark green of the forest. The caddies pointed that out to us as we teed off and discovered additionally that the green was protected by a small pond and four bunkers. Secondly, the tenth, again from an elevated tee, is a fabulous driving hole with the fairway well defined by huge trees. Between the tenth and eleventh is a wonderful halfway house which offers a much needed break, followed by a classic short par four, the eleventh. One must drive over a severe bunker with more of the same to the right and punitive heather rough. Third and last, the fourteenth is the longest hole on the course with classic cross bunkering and a hidden bunker to the right of the green and the fifteenth, a 230 yard par three, frequently requires a driver and is bunkered short on the right with several others on the left.

From the early twentieth century, Sunningdale Old was well recognized. Starting in 1903 it hosted the World Match Play four times, the British Masters in the 1940's and 1950's and most notably the 1987 Walker Cup. It has hosted the British Womens Open and the European Open four times, and most recently in 2009 and 2015 the Senior British Open. Bobby Jones was no stranger to this course and had a great fondness for it. He had an almost perfect score of 66 in one of his two qualifying rounds for the 1926 Open Championship, a tournament he won at Lytham & St. Annes. His card, in shooting the 66, showed nothing but 3's and 4's with 33 putts. This was unheard of in 1926 and Bernard Darwin summed up Jones' round as "incredible indecent". I have Sunningdale Old Course listed fifty-fourth in my list of favorites.

Wentworth Club, West Course, Virginia Waters, Surrey, England

The Wentworth Club has its origins from a noble estate belonging to the Wentworths. In 1922 a builder and developer, W. G. Tarrent, acquired the development rights for the property and patterned the property after St. George's Hill, Weybridge. Tarrent immediately employed Harry Colt to design the East course in 1924 and the more famous West course in 1926. The Club has had several owners and its ups and downs based on the economy, but suffice it to say that it has survived with flying colors as the Club is surrounded by and entwined with the Wentworth Estate. This area is one of the most expensive real estate developments in the London suburbs. Most recently in 2014, the Beijing-based Reignwood Investments has acquired the property and has caused an uproar by substantially raising the dues and initiation fees.

The Club has three 18 hole courses and an executive nine hole course. The East Course opened in 1922 and the Edinburgh Course, designed by John Jacobs, in 1990. I will not discuss these other two courses as we did not see them during our visit in April, 1997.

Bernard Darwin feels The West Course is a cross between primarily heather and a parkland, tree lined course. The first hole is a relatively benign par four which most of us will recognize as Wentworth has been highly televised. The second is an exacting 155 yard par three with a huge oak between two bunkers to the right of the green. The third is a brutally long, uphill par four. When we played here in 1997 my foursome consisted of the aforementioned William McKee and Blake Griffith along with Perry Soder, an Atlanta radiologist. On three William belted a drive of 280 plus yards and the caddies looked on in disbelief. Whereupon Blake yelled in our southern drawl: "He's just a bleached out Tiger Woods." All eight of us laughed for the next two holes. In reminiscing about this fun time, it's sad to think that I was far from the oldest member of this group yet the other three have left this earth: kinda encourages one to adopt the mentality of living each day to the fullest. I can assure you that all members of that foursome lived that way.

The thirteenth is another of Colt's long par fours. A long dogleg left, the right side is protected by a strategically placed bunker and the par should be a five, as it is for the ladies. The seventeenth is a long severe par five that sweeps left seemingly endlessly. The tee shot is daunting, between tall pines, very similar to the eighteenth at Augusta. Ernie Els, a prominent member and part time resident, revised The West in 2006 pushing the yardage to over 7,300 yards and adding thirty bunkers.

As previously mentioned, it's the most televised course in the UK having been the host of the HSBC World Match Play Championship from 1964 to 2007 and the BMW European PGA Tournament since 1984. The 1953 Ryder Cup, which was held here, was one of the most hotly contested matches ever. Lloyd Mangram was captain for America and Henry Cotton for Great Britain. The match came down to the last two games when Peter Alliss made double bogey on eighteen allowing Jim Teraesa to win a point. Following that, Bernard Hunt missed a putt on eighteen for a half with Dave Douglas. The US won 61/2 to 51/2.

When we visited Surrey in 1997 there was an ongoing severe drought and the only course that was watered was Wentworth. I understand that, because it hosts the WGC European PGA Championship, it is constantly in good shape and nothing is spared, including water to keep it that way. I have rated Wentworth ninety-ninth in my list of favorites.

The Berkshire Golf Club, Blue Course,
Ascot, England

The Berkshire Golf Club was founded in 1928 on Crown lands originally used by Queen Ann for hunting parties in the seventeenth and eighteenth centuries. Both the Blue and the Red were developed and built simultaneously and designed by Herbert Fowler, a noted golf architect in the early and mid twentieth century. He designed numerous courses in central and south England including Beau Desert, Stafford-shire, Crystal Springs in Burlingame, Eastward Ho! in Chatham and both the East and West Saunton Golf Club Courses in Devon. Probably his best known course is Walton Heath in Surrey as we will discuss forthwith.

The Berkshire Golf Club, Red Course, Ascot, England

The Red Course has always had the highest ranking of the two, checking in at 34 in Golf World's rankings of courses in Britain and Ireland, with the Blue ranked at 55 in the same publication. I believe the Blue was closed for competition or maintenance the day we visited. Even so, the Red was more than enough course for us in difficulty and scenery, with the fairways lined with beautiful pine trees and heather ground cover. The Red is strange in that both the first and tenth are par threes. The first is a testimony of things to come with the green on a hump over 200 yards away. There is trouble short right and long left to punish both the slice and hook respectively. This hole holds the distinction of being the signature hole on this if not both courses. The front is probably the easier of the two nines with two relatively short par fives. The tenth is a beautiful hole with mounds forming both sand and grass bunkers to the green. The incoming nine finishes with five strong par fours, the best or worst of which is a long dogleg with a bunker cut into the corner of the dogleg.

We had a great time here listening to Mr. Griffith's comments regarding the preserved area of barbed wire and solid steel rods placed on the fairways during World War II to prevent German planes from landing in the open spaces. I do not have the Red in my list of favorites, but one comment I made in my Journal is that I would like to come back here as it is hardly more than twenty miles from south-central

London, and a stone's throw from Heathrow. Consider it next time you fly into that busy airport.

Walton Heath The Old Course, Walton on the Hill, Tadworth, England

Walton Heath Old is one of the oldest and most historic courses in this area of England. Founded in 1904, it was the first design by W. Herbert Fowler, who we mentioned above. When we played here in 1997, England was in the midst of a severe drought and the course, being flat, was as hard as concrete. As I recall, the tees from which we played, accounted for that by making the course stretch well beyond the 6,400 yards ordinarily used for visitors. The Championship layout measures 7,464 yards. We were all driving the ball downwind 250 plus yards with Blake and William topping out at well over 340 yards. A little known fact, brought out by one of our caddies, is that Herb Fowler is credited with redesigning the 18th at Pebble Beach Golf Links. It seems that he was brought to Carmel to redo the Del Monte Golf Course in 1922. While there he made some suggestions regarding Pebble Beach, but they were ignored. The next year, complaints were made regarding the par four finishing hole at Pebble lacking character. The owners brought out Mr. Fowler's suggestion adding almost 200 yards to the hole; that's how it was transformed from a 379 yard par four to a 548 par five.

The course is a heathland beauty, built in fields of purple heather with sandy soil and crisp turf. James Braid was the first and only pro until 1950. It has the unique distinction of having a reigning monarch, Edward VIII as a captain and four Prime Ministers as members. Those are: Lloyd George, Bonar Law, Arthur Balfour and Winston Churchill. The Old has played host to numerous tournaments in England, but the highlights have to be the 1981 Ryder Cup and recently the Senior Open Championship.

Like its older sister, Berkshire Blue, it starts out with a long par three. The par four second and fifth are demanding holes with the former sweeping down into a valley and the latter demanding a straight drive to avoid the heather that is everywhere. The incoming nine starts out fairly benign, but beginning with the short, sharp dogleg right par 4 twelfth, the trouble starts. The 13th, 14th and 16th are long par fives, combined with a punishing par four 15th that plays into the prevailing wind, making for one of the longest four hole stretches of any championship course. The par three seventeenth plays over a valley to a raised "island" green. The "island" is defined by a raised green with sand bunkers surrounding it. The straight eighteenth, with fairway bunkers to the left and a cross bunker just short of the green, completes the picture. One other comment is that, in contrast to most courses, the greens are not raised but are just a continuation of the fairway, making run-up shots a must and high iron shots difficult to hold the green. I have it rated one hundred and twenty-first in my list of favorites.

West Hill Golf Club, Woking, Surrey, England.

This Club was founded in 1909 and the course design is attributed to Cuthbert Butchart who became the first professional. The course has remained relatively the same one that Butchart designed except for bunker refurbishment and revision of the tees. The latter is a great improvement to frame each hole between the massive, mature pines and the purple heather, providing a colorful ribbon outside of the fairways. The course is relatively short by today's standards, measuring 6,338 yards from the championship tees and 6,060 yards from the daily tees. The outward nine has three par threes and one par five, turning in 34, and the back has one par five and two par threes for a par of 69. The course as such was right up my alley in that we were required to play as twosomes. I got off to a good start in my match and with all the bets won 100 pounds. I can assure you, I had lost more than that in the other five days of play.

Caddies were important as the tee shots needed to be carefully directed to the right place to avoid the forest of pines and heather rough. The first hole was memorable because of the overhanging pine branches on the right. The fifth, a par five, is possible to reach in two for the long hitter, but anyone taking that chance must risk leaving his ball in the band of heather that crosses the fairway over a hill and in front of the green.

The ninth is memorable in that the 170 yard par three has bunkers that guard the narrow entrance, major trouble off the back and a three-tiered green to contend with. The three finishing holes are probably the best as the sixteenth requires a straight tee shot through an avenue of trees to a flat well bunkered green, the par five seventeenth is all about avoiding the bunkers on all three initial shots here and the eighteenth is a good par four demanding two good shots with an out-of-bounds behind the green and another three-tiered green to contend with. I do not have West Hills listed in my list of favorites; it's just too narrow.

Further south to the coast of England lie three courses that I have yet to visit.
1. Royal St. George or Sandwich is the only course in The Open rota that I have not played. I have a good friend, Tom Dowden, who is a longstanding member and although I had a recent invitation, our schedules always seem to be misaligned.
2. Royal Cinque Ports Golf Club is located in the town of Deal. The course also goes simply by the name of Deal. Assuming that you are like me, if you are still reading you probably are, you are curious regarding the name. The name is derived from an ancient group of trading towns granted special trading privileges by the ruling medieval monarchs known as "Cinque Ports".
3. Rye Golf Club is located in East Sussex on the coast due south of London. The course was started in 1893 on and among the Camber sandhills; it has ideal links land winding up, down and around the high dunes. I really want to see Rye and the other two courses mentioned above.

Part II
The North-West of England

A friend at Wade Hampton suggested, since I love links golf so much, I must go to this area of England to at least play the three courses that are in The Open rota. On discussing this with several Wade Hampton members, I found that we had at least two members of Royal Liverpool or "Hoylake" (as most locals call this course), and Royal Lytham & St. Annes. That got me hooked on planning a trip there with three of my best friends: Dr. Tom Fleischer, an orthopedic surgeon who sadly died at the young age of 57, Morgan Fayssoux from Greenville and Dr. Dick Vann.

Mainly because of this lineup, the itinerary had to be a ten as this was a wild and crazy crowd and picky. The gateway city is Manchester and after a flight there we were set to play Wallasey, another course in this area, at three pm.

But I had my marching orders from my children and Faye to get 200 pounds of Jack Nicklaus five pound notes for gifts. So first we stopped at a bank in Ellesmere Port; I went in to change money and get the five pound notes. We were all changing money into pounds and I, initially innocently, remarked that I had a two pounder in my pocket, meaning a two pound coin. Well the female teller and two ladies waiting behind me all burst out laughing. Not one to let a good time go to waste, I continued by asking her if she wanted to see it. Her response was a priceless "oh-oh not here" and I countered by saying" maybe outside." Other than my friends, the other eight or so people present were females and all were laughing so hard that many of them were crying. So much for being politically correct, but the trip was off to a roaring start.

Wallasey Golf Club,Wirral, England.

This course and Royal Liverpool are located on The Wirral peninsula, a spit of land just west of Liverpool, England. The other courses are north of that city, all basically along the coast. In 1891 Tom Morris Sr., initially designed this course. After a survey he reported to the founders: "at Wallasey there are all the conditions at hand to form a classic links course". That's about like asking Colonel Sanders what type of meat he likes to eat. It is certainly a classic links layout playing through and on sand dunes and on tight running fairways. Over the years Harold Hilton, four times The Champion Golfer of the Year and James Braid, five times with the same honor and Frederick Hawtree all had the opportunity of renovating the course. Most recently, Donald Steel oversaw improvements to it.

Even if you pass up playing here, and I'm not recommending that you should, at least stop in and see the portrait of Bobby Jones by the Wallasey member J.A.A.Berrie painted after Jones qualified for The Open here in 1930. Of course that was the "Grand Slam" year when he won The Open at nearby Hoylake. The other claim to fame for Wallasey is that Dr. Frank Stableford devised the Stableford scoring system when a member here. As far as I am concerned, he could have forgotten it. Maybe it was because the caddies didn't show, the long flight over from Atlanta, or the fact that it has taken five course architects to get it right, but I do not have this course rated in my list of favorites.

Royal Liverpool Golf Club "Hoylake", Wirral, England

Founded in 1869 it received "Royal" designation in 1871 due to the patronage of the Duke of Connaught. Robert Chambers, one of Queen Victoria's younger sons, and George Morris (younger brother of Old Tom Morris) were commissioned to lay out the original course. The course was extended to 18 holes in 1871 and Harry Colt redesigned it early in the 20th century.

Located on the northwest corner of the Wirral Peninsula, it is a classic links course. Hoylake has been a leader in amateur golf, hosting the first Men's Amateur Championship in 1885, the first ever match between Scotland and England in 1902, and the first transatlantic match between Great Britain and Ireland and the United States in 1921. This match is now recognized as the inaugural Walker Cup Match.

Three other names in amateur golf resonate with Hoylake: John Ball who won the Amateur Championship eight times between 1888 and 1912, and The Open Championship in 1890; Harold Hilton whose record was just as impressive as he won The Open twice, in 1892 and 1897. Of course the third amateur in this list is Bobby Jones who, as you already know won The Open here in 1930 on his way to the "Grand Slam", as an Amateur. Hoylake was omitted in The Open rota after 1967, but in 2006 and 2014 hosted this most prestigious tournament with winners Tiger Woods, hitting stingers, in the former and Rory McIlroy overpowering everyone in the latter.

The course starts flat with the infamous first, a dogleg right with an out-of-bounds on the right all the way to the green. Indeed players in both 2006 and 2014 played way left to avoid this hazard, found two to three yards off the putting surface. The second, another par four, is the only remaining original hole in Tom Morris's layout. The third, fourth and sixth head toward the Irish Sea, while seven and eight head south adjacent to the holes headed back north hard by the ocean. The ninth, tenth, eleventh and twelfth are directly on the beach before the routing turns back inland. The outgoing nine has a par of 36, while the incoming nine's par is 36, with three long finishing holes to deal with, especially tough on short hitters like myself. Indeed in the last two Opens played here, the seventeenth par four became the first and the normal eighteenth, another par four, became the second, leaving the long par five sixteenth as the finishing hole. I have this course rated ninety fourth in my list of favorites.

Royal Birkdale Golf Club, Southport, Merseyside, England

This is, in my opinion, the "must play" venue in North West England. The Club was founded in 1889 and moved to its present location in Birkdale Hills in 1894. Three generations of Hawtree golf architects have had a hand in its design. Frederick G. Hawtree and J.H. Taylor designed the original tract and the routing. Frederick W., son of the former, made some modifications in the 1960's; in 1993 Martin Hawtree, his son, modernized the course and rebuilt the greens. Birkdale has hosted two Ryder Cups, in 1965 and again in 1969. The latter was the scene of one of the greatest displays of sportsmanship ever recorded in a game that is known for sportsmanship. Jack Nicklaus conceded a difficult, three foot putt to Tony Jacklin to half their final match. As defending champions, the US retained the Cup with a 16-16 tie. Not everyone was happy with this "concession" as the act is now referred to, not the least of which was Sam Snead who was the Captain of the US Team. Nicklaus and Jacklin have fairly recently jointly designed a course outside of Sarasota, Florida appropriately named The Concession.

Royal Birkdale has hosted The Open eight times with the likes of Arnold Palmer, Lee Trevino and Peter

Thomson having won there. The most recent winner there in 2008 was Padraig Harrington. The course has also hosted two Womens British Opens, in 1982 and in 1986. The course layout follows the valleys between very large dunes which are the most spectacular aspect of the course. (Figure 34) This

Figure 34. The par three seventh hole at Birkdale has the eighth fairway behind it and the towering dunes beyond, protecting the course from the Irish Sea.

design makes for excellent spectator conditions and explains why the Royal & Ancient, golf's ruling body in the UK, considers this course a favorite for The Open. The course starts out slightly inland with three brutal par fours followed by the fourth, a 200 yard par three. Five heads to the beach with the Irish Sea as a backdrop and the sixth, seventh and eighth tees are adjacent to the ocean. The twelfth, a 145 yard par three, follows the beach and is a spectacular hole.

The finish is somewhat bizarre; seventeen and eighteen are par fives, ending a hard incoming nine with par at 37.

I should mention that playing always includes betting. In betting on the outcome of a golf match, we divide up two players versus the other two for ten dollars or pounds, as the location would dictate. We then play what is known as match play, with each team winning, losing or halving a hole. When the match is decided and one team has won, (the long match) and yet there are still holes to play, we begin another match, (the short match) typically for half the amount of the long match. The players decide the teams in any number of ways, but frequently it's the lower and higher handicapped players against the other two. At Royal Birkdale, Fleischer, the low handicapped man and I, the higher man, were paired together and we were closed out 5 & 4 after fourteen. That means that we had lost the long match 5 down with 4 holes to play, so we started another match. During that short match my score of six with a stroke means I made a five on the par five, fifteenth and we won the hole and subsequently the short bet over Fayssoux and Vann.

The clubhouse is Art Deco circa 1935. It is designed to look like a ship floating on a sea of dunes, but looks like it would be better suited for South Beach, Miami rather than North West England. The Club's Royal designation was granted by HRH George VI, November 11, 1951 and as such was among one of his last decrees, as he died less than three months later on February 6,1952. His successor HRH Elizabeth II still reigns going on now sixty-four years later. I have it rated sixty-third in my list of favorites.

Formby Golf Club, Formby, Liverpool, England

We were all pleasantly surprised by the quality and playability of this course. Other than "The Royals" it was the best we played on what is known as England's Golf Coast. Located south of Southport and slightly northwest of Liverpool, it is certainly worth a visit. Founded in 1884 and originally laid out by Willie Park, James Braid changed the original layout of fifteen through eighteen in 1922 when erosion of the shoreline along the eighth and ninth greens threatened these holes. The erosion was caused by both the dredging in the Liverpool port and the regular gale force winds that blow there. Donald Steel redesigned these holes and at the same time shortened the tenth to a par three. This new hole is sheltered in pines surrounding the hole and at 178 yards is a very difficult par three.

The whole course is composed of rolling dunes land with variations in terrain, which is sometimes tree lined and tight and sometimes bordered by heather. One constant is that this course is usually battered by wind and if you don't have a knockdown shot you are out of luck. The elevated tee on the long par four ninth gives one a panoramic view of the Mersey River and Liverpool Bay, which on a clear day is worth the price of admission. Despite all of the above I've not rated it in my list of favorites, because when we played it the course was in poor condition with unkept areas.

The Southport & Ainsdale Golf Club Ltd., Ainsdale, Southport, England

Founded as a nine hole course in 1906, S & A, as it is referred to, was composed of both male and female members in marked contrast to other clubs of its time. George Lowe, the Lytham professional, laid out three more holes and refined the original nine in 1907. In 1925 after moving to a new clubhouse, the Club hired James Braid to design six holes which had been lost in the move, and to remodel the original twelve holes. They remain virtually intact since that remodeling.

The main claim to fame at S & A is their hosting of two Ryder Cup Matches. In the first, held in 1933, the US team captained by Walter Hagan, lost the Cup on the last putt of the last match on the last hole. It's just a shame that the BBC couldn't televise it! Samuel Ryder coach, Abe Mitchell whose figure is believed to adorn the top of the trophy, won thirteen of the last fourteen holes to assist in the British victory. S & A hosted the Ryder Cup four years later in 1937, and with a much less exciting finish, the US won handily 8 points to 4.

S & A is set amongst ranges of tall sandhills and smaller dunes. The course ambles through tall pines and mounds defining the fairways. Par is 70 with both nines having par at 35. Likewise both nines start with a par three. The eighth par three, "Plateau", could be the signature hole but isn't. (Figure 35) James Braid usually chose one hole that he put his name on and the par four third is his namesake here. The tee is markedly elevated with a panoramic view of the Irish Sea and inland for fifty miles on a clear day.

Figure 35. The eighth hole at Southport & Ainsdale
defined by the high dunes

The only par five on the incoming nine is the sixteenth, "Gumbleys", with a blind second shot and a
guarding cross bunker to catch the second shot. In
our match here, my partner Fleischer and I, had been
getting beat regularly by Fayssoux's and Vann's good
play. We were one up on this hole when Morgan cold
topped his second shot 50 yards. Tom had spoke
earlier with "we've got the SOB's here." Wrong!
Fayssoux followed up with a three wood to three feet
from the cup and made the putt for a birdie. The
match ended up halved after my 4 for 3 on seventeen
and Vann's birdie on the eighteenth. You could not
script a better or more fun finish among friends. I do
not, however, have S & A rated in my list of favorites.

Hillside Golf Club Ltd., Hillside, Southport, England

The course, designed by Fred Hawtree in 1962 is a relatively new course by English standards. It also is a tale of two nines, with the outgoing flat and bland, and the incoming set in high dunes, defined by large pines and laid out with mounds lining the fairways. As such this nine is probably the best nine holes on the "English Golf Coast". It is located adjacent to Royal Birkdale on its north, and is immediately adjacent to Birkdale's eighteenth hole.

Figure 36. The par three tenth at Hillside framed by dunes and pines and illustrating what is to come on the beautiful incoming nine

Both nines have a par of 36 and if the truth be told the par threes and fives make this course more interesting than the somewhat dull two shotters. From the Medal tees, all par fives are over 500 yards and from the men's tees, this course measures 6,578 yards. We played it from the senior tees measuring 6,200 yards and it was plenty of course even for our single digit player. The par three seventh is framed by pines, as is the signature par three tenth. (Figure 36) Despite this great incoming tract, I do not have it in my list of favorites, because the front nine holes is flat and bland.

Royal Lytham & St. Annes Golf Club, Lytham St. Annes, Lancashire, England.

The Club, founded in 1886, was moved to its present location when George Lowe oversaw construction of this links in 1898. The layout remains essentially intact, except in 1919 Harry Colt repositioned some of the greens and tees and added bunkers, not that the bunkers were needed; as of last count there were more that 385 of the nasty little devils. I was in so many of them that the guys suggested I trade my bucket hat for a turban. Royal Lytham & St. Annes has hosted eleven Opens, two Ryder Cups, and most recently in 2015, The Walker Cup Matches. The course is surrounded by suburban housing and the requisite railroad line and, despite being a links course, is not close to the sea. The sea breezes, however, still have a tremendous influence on the play here.

Bobby Jones qualified for the 1926 Open here by shooting 66-68 for a two round total of 134 at Sunningdale. His 66 is considered by many to be the nearest thing to a perfect round ever played. After the second round here, in 1926, Jones was tied with Walter Hagan at 144. An American, Al Watrous, was paired with Jones on the final day of play on Friday. Watrous was two shots ahead after the third round on Friday morning. In the afternoon's final round, he held that lead with five holes to play, then Jones made a miraculous charge and on seventeen, took over the lead with a wonderful mashie (five iron) shot from hard packed sand. Despite a charge by Hagan, Jones won by two over Watrous. It was 26 years later before The Open was again held here. In 1952 Bobby Locke braved gale force winds to win an exciting tournament over Peter Thomson by one and Fred Daly by four. To briefly finish the scoring history at Lytham & St. Annes, Tony Jacklin won by two shots over Bob Charles in 1969.

The course at Lytham & St. Annes is fairly flat and predictable. The first is a long par three with heavy rough and bunkers surrounding it. This is about as big as the sand dunes get on this layout. (Figure 37) The second and third run parallel to a railroad track that is out-of-bounds on two, three, seven, eight and nine; so do not slice it here. The outgoing nine is downwind, with the incoming nine generally playing into the prevailing wind. This makes for a challenging and exciting finish to any Open played here.Certainly that was the case in 2012. The last five holes are all long par fours, except sixteen at 372 yards. Adam Scott, in search of his first major victory, was four strokes ahead of Ernie Els with four holes to play after a birdie at fourteen. He then uncharacteristically bogeyed the last four only to lose by one stroke to Els who had birdied the eighteenth.

I hadn't had Lytham & St. Annes rated in my list of favorites, but out of deference to my friends who are members here and the R&A, I have recently listed it 124 in my list of favorites.

Figure 37. The first, par three, at Lytham St. Annes illustrating the numerous hazards surrounding this hole

The St. Annes Old Links Golf Club, St. Annes-on-Sea, Lancashire, England

This course and Club, founded in 1901, is set in a dense residential area and reminds me of the train ride into London from Gatwick. If you want a flat lie, which for one who has played most of my golf at Wade Hampton is unknown to me, this course is for you. It's about as flat as the drive from Denver Airport to Mullen, Nebraska, the location of Sand Hills. Having said all of that, I really would not recommend playing this course. The only saving grace is the picturesque ninth, ending in a very long, elevated green with great bunkers guarding the perimeter. The eighteenth, a par five, is a nice finishing hole and good spot to take a final photograph of the group on this trip. (Figure 38) Obviously I do not have "Old Links" rated.

Figure 38. The fearless foursome on eighteenth fairway at The St. Annes Old Links Golf Club. Left to right: Dick Vann, Tom Fleischer, the author and Morgan Fayssoux

Sample Itineraries for Golf in England

Obviously it will take two trips to cover the ground I have outlined in the third chapter.

The first itinerary I would choose is to the south of London. Fly either to Gatwick or Heathrow. The former is south of London and the latter is west. Again, I would fly on Saturday evening to either gateway city airport.

1. If you are west I would definitely play Walton Heath on the day of arrival.

2. Play Sunningdale Old Course the second day.

3. Play Wentworth West on the third day, and maybe a second round on either of The Berkshire Courses.

4. Travel south and play Rye the fourth day.

5. Play Royal St. George's the fifth day.

6. Play Royal Clique Ports (Deal) the sixth day.

7. If you skipped the second round on the third day, play The Berkshire Courses coming back north.

8. Assuming you flew over on Saturday night, fly back the following Sunday.

The second itinerary to the north-west of England would be to fly Manchester, England Saturday night.

1. I would try to book either Hillside or Southport & Ainsdale the arrival day, i.e. Sunday. Those are the closest courses to Manchester other than Royal Lytham & St. Annes.

2. Play Royal Lytham & St. Annes on the next day.

3. Play either Hillside or S & A or both on the third day or Tuesday, assuming you didn't get in a round on the day of arrival.

4. Play Royal Birkdale the following day or Wednesday.

5. Go down to the Whirral Peninsular Wednesday and stay at the Thornton House Hotel.

6. Play Royal Liverpool (Hoylake) on Thursday.

If I had to do this trip over again, and if you are aggressive and do not think you are worn out, I would venture into Wales. The closest two great courses are Nefyan & District and Royal St. Davids. I would arrange to play those two courses on Friday and Saturday and get back to Manchester to fly home Sunday. That's seven courses in seven days.

Rankings of the Fifteen courses played in England

1. Sunningdale Old Course, # 54.

2. Royal Birkdale Golf Club, # 63.

3. Royal Liverpool (Hoylake) Golf Club, #94.

4. Wentworth Golf Club (West Course), # 99.

5. Walton Heath Golf Club, # 121.

6. Royal Lytham & St. Annes, # 124.

7. The Berkshire Golf Club (Red Course).

8. Hillside Golf Club.

9. Formby Golf Club.

10. West Hills Golf Club.

11. Hampton Court Park Palace Golf Club.

12. Southport & Ainsdale Golf Club.

13. Wallasey Golf Club.

14. Foxhills Golf Club Longcross Course.

15. The St. Annes Old Links Golf Club.

Chapter IV

Europe

I do not know of any venue in Europe that is a "must do" location for golf. The possible exception to this statement is Valderrama, the Augusta of Europe, in southern Spain. Now known as Real (Royal) Valderrama, it was an average golf course designed by R.T. Jones, Sr. but transformed by industrialist billionaire, Jamie Ortiz-Patino into the highest rated course in Europe. Its claim to fame was hosting the 1997 Ryder Cup. The US was captained by Tom Kite and his counterpart couldn't be a more opposite character, Seve Ballesteros. Aided by some home cooking by Seve, and perhaps too because his team had played the course numerous times, and no doubt a stellar performance by five rookies from Europe, the home team prevailed 141/2 - 131/2. I have not had the opportunity to play it.

I have had two opportunities to play golf for a week in Europe: One in the Algarve region of Portugal and the other on a Kalos river cruise down the Rhine River. I enjoyed each trip immensely, primarily because of the people we were with from Wade Hampton. Would I recommend going? Well no, because there are much better places to go in the US, UK, Ireland, and other golf resorts worldwide. Since I'm a bit non-plussed with European golf, I have not rated any of the eleven courses I've played in my super list.

Part I
Algarve, Portugal

The Algarve area, translated, 'the West', is the southernmost region of mainland Portugal, with the Atlantic Ocean on the west, the Mediterranean Sea on the south and Spain to the east. It only took William McKee, previously mentioned, two months after returning from our first Rendezvous trip to Ireland to read an article featuring the cliffs and ravines of Vale do Lobo Golf Club and he was well on

Figure 39. Map of Portugal with the Algarve area in the south

his way to planning our second trip. Of course seven of the eight couples from the first wonderful trip gladly followed in April 1994. The gateway city is Faro, Portugal the largest city in the Algarve region. (Figure 39.)

Vale do Lobo Golf Club, Royal Course, Algarve, Portugal.

Our first outing here was on the original course in the Algarve region designed by Sir Henry Cotton in 1966. It was recently revised by American architect Rocky Roquemore. The outward nine is a parkland layout that takes one on a stroll on fairways lined with umbrella pines and fig trees, dotted with lakes on it. The outward nine then terminates at the virtual island ninth green. The inward nine is more dramatic with distant views of the cliff-lined coast from twelve, thirteen and fourteen. The most dramatic sixteenth runs along ocean ravines atop high cliffs that fall to the beach below. The photographs of this hole definitely attracted us to the beauties of this region which has become the symbol of golf in the Algarve. The Royal Course here measures 6,655 yards from the tips, 6,215 from the member tees and 5,418 from the ladies' tees.

Vale do Lobo, Ocean Course, Algarve, Portugal

This Course was was not completed when we visited in 1994. My understanding is that four holes are on the Mediterranean Sea and it has less elevation between the course and the beach than the Royal Course. These courses have hosted the Portuguese Open and both offer a unique golf experience here.

*Quinto do Lago Resort and Golf Club,
Algarve, Portugal*

There are now three courses in this extensive beach resort and golf destination. The hotel is set just inland from a barrier island with a wonderfully expansive, essentially deserted, beach. The hotel was our home for the six days while we were here, and I cannot think of a better location for a golf tour to this area. The recently developed Laranjal Course (2009) was voted the best new course in Portugal. Built on an old orangery, it features huge fast greens and Augusta styled bunkers.

*Quinto do Lago Resort, South Course,
Algarve, Portugal*

The flagship course of this resort is the South Course. It was the brainchild of Andre Jordan when he visited this region in 1970. Set amongst 2,000 acres of the beautiful Ria Formosa Natural Park, he developed the resort and then opened the South Course in 1974. This course, along with four holes on the North Course, were designed by William Mitchell. The parkland layout weaves among umbrella pines, several lakes and a plethora of wild flowers. It has hosted the Portuguese Open eight times, the most notable in 1989 when Colin Montgomerie won the first of his 24 wins on the European Tour by shooting a course record of 63 in the last round.

Quinto do Lago North Course, Algarve, Portugal

When we were here in April of 1994, this was probably the worst course we played. It is relatively flat and lacked memorable holes. That all changed when Beau Welling, whose parents live and play at Wade Hampton, teamed up with Paul McGinley, the former Ryder Cup Captain, and redesigned a tight new course. The narrow fairways demand precise shots. Since I haven't played this renovated course, I will not comment further except to say that it was voted as the best new course in Europe in 2014.

Our travel agent, along with William McKee, made sure we had local nightly entertainment at a hacienda overlooking the beach and the small town surrounding Quinto do Lago Resort. We were thoroughly entertained with barbecues of exotic meats, vocal performers, comedy and other local bands and lastly Portuguese wines, wines and more wines. The Portuguese vintages may not be recognized as the best in the world but they were good and relatively cheap. The two nights we were entertained at the hacienda, everyone danced, drank and were very, very merry. That's exactly what a vacation should be!

Vila Sol Golf Club, Algarve, Portugal.

Designed by Donald Steel and opened for play in 1991, Vila Sol's first two nine holes, now known as Prime and Challenge, have been supplemented by another nine, the Prestige. The course fits into the original undulating landscape. The fairways wind through the ever present umbrella pines, fig and cork trees. The man-made lakes seem to be a little bit overdone, but do produce esthetically pleasing hazards.

The opening holes are brutal, with three par fours all measuring well over four hundred yards. The seventh is a 198 yard par three that is book-ended by two par fives. The incoming nine is shorter but much narrower, making it at least as difficult as the outgoing nine. Vila Sol has hosted the Portuguese Open twice, in 1992 and 1993, and is probably the reason William picked it for us to play in 1994.

Vilamoura I Golf Club, Algarve, Portugal

Sometime after we played here in 1994, a golf course management firm, Oceanico, bought this original layout and has turned the property and hotel into a mega golf resort. There are six other courses in this consortium, some of which carry the name of the architect. Vilamoura I is now Oceanico Old Course. The others are Oceanico Victoria, designed by The Arnold Palmer Group, Laguna by Joe Lee, Pinhal, the second course here, designed by Frank Pennick, Millennium by the Hawktree & Sons firm, along with the Faldo and the O'Connor Jr. courses.

So Vilamoural I course, now named Oceanico Old Course, was designed by Frank Pennick in 1969, and as such is one of the oldest courses in the Algarve area. It is a perfect example of a parkland layout with umbrella pines lining the fairways, and encroaching on them, if you ask me. This course starts out with three straightaway holes, two par fours and a par five. The fourth is the signature hole with the only water hazard on the course and a huge umbrella pine directly between the tee and green on this bizarre par three hole. The remaining holes run back and forth across essentially flat terrain and as such are not very memorable; the only real hazards are the umbrella pines which are everywhere.

San Lorenzo Golf Club, Algarve, Portugal

Just behind a barrier island on the Mediterranean Sea is San Lorenzo Golf Club. Constantly ranked in the top thirty courses in Europe, it was ranked third when we visited it in 1994. It was not included in our itinerary, but once we heard about it we booked a couple of rooms at the Dona Filipa Hotel just to be able to play the course.

The course is built around a lake formed by the Ria Formosa Nature Reserve and Estuary. The eighteen holes of San Lorenzo run through a wide variety of scenic locations measuring over 6,800 yards. The first four holes run over fairly steeply undulating land heavily encrusted with, you guessed it, umbrella pine. The par three fifth opens up to stunning views of the lake and beach beyond. Beginning at the eighth hole the layout is adjacent to a brackish water lake which comes into play on this hole, as well as the ninth, tenth, sixteenth, seventeenth and eighteenth, all of which circumnavigate the lake. The views across the Ria Formosa are wonderful. The last green is essentially an island and is a dramatic climax to a very good golf course.

This book was in the final stages of editing when, while eating breakfast at Wade Hampton, a friend asked me if I had recounted the story about Monte Carlo, which Blake loved to tell. I had a physician friend in Montgomery who owned a villa on the French Riviera. He had recommended that Faye and I stay at the Hotel du Cap Eden-Roc. I knew it was expensive but we were in for a real shock. Blake and

Susan Griffith, along with William and Anne McKee,
joined us for an after trip additional trip. After a 250
dollar limousine ride to the hotel we decided to rent a
nice van for transportation.

We did the usual sightseeing venues including San
Tropez and Monte Carlo going over on the Middle
Cornish and back along the Grand Cornish. Blake
was in agony on this high road. At first I thought he
was joking, as he frets a lot, and "just being Blake"
until William said that he was genuinely afraid of
heights. Well, the men decided that we should return
that evening and gamble. We dressed up, went back
over on the Lower Cornish and after dinner in Monte
Carlo, went to the casino. We entered the under-
ground parking garage and took the usual ticket for
entry. All signage was in French and Italian so we
didn't have a clue about what do do when the boys
were finished trying their luck mainly on the Roulette
Wheel.

When we exited the garage a gate was, as usual,
blocking our exit. Those signs that we saw everywhere advised us to pay the parking charge before
returning to our vehicle. Of course, we couldn't read
the French and Italian. and didn't validate our ticket.
The French attendant was running around shouting to
us in French and Italian and we understood nothing.
Finally we got the word billet, which rang a bell I
handed a ticket in my pocket to Faye, who was
driving, and she stuck it in the meter, instead of the
parking ticket it was a laundry ticket and it gummed
up the machine. By then there was a line of cars
behind us: Mercedes, was the cheapest one,
Bentleys, a Ferrari or two and a Lamborghini, all
blowing their horns. The Frenchman was still running

around, waving his hands and cursing but had no option but to let us out manually. You would have had to be there to appreciate how funny this was, in our rental, no-name van too.

Part II
The Rhine River Valley

The Rhine River's headwaters start in the Swiss Alps and end in the North Sea with The Netherlands delta marking the termination point. At 820 miles long, it is the second longest river in Europe behind only the Danube. It flows north by Basel in northern Switzerland, and forms the border between France and Germany before passing Amsterdam and ending in the North Sea. (Figure 40) We traveled up river flying into Amsterdam and back from Zurich. Blake Griffith, Fritz Alders and I tried to go over early and spend a day in Amsterdam, but our wives thought better of that. To quote them: "we may have been born at night, but in was not last night"!

The trip was all arranged by Kalos Golf River Cruises and the planning was impeccable with every detail carefully worked out, down to trucking golf carts to the course sites for us spoiled Americans. Along with the Alders, Griffiths and Kitchens, there were nine other couples from Wade Hampton on this trip taken from July 9th to the 18th, 2004. As mentioned earlier, close friends make any trip much more enjoyable. The opening day tour of Amsterdam, reclaimed land in Holland and the Van Gogh art in both the Rijksmuseum and Kroller Muller Museums was a

Figure 40. The Course of the Rhine River through
Western Europe

great start to the cruise. The non-golfing members
also enjoyed the various outings to castles, cathedrals
and other sites along this historic river's banks.

Gut Larchenhof Golf Club, Cologne, Germany.

The first and probably the best layout of the trip was
Gut Larchenhof, the only signature Jack Nicklaus
course in Germany. Located just 15 miles northwest
of Cologne, the layout opened in 1997. Its primary
claim to fame is that the course had hosted The
European PGA Tour's Linde German Masters from

1998-2005. Most recently it had hosted the
Mercedes-Benz Championship from 2007 to 2009,
and again in 2016. The Club, in contrast to most
other courses in Germany, has taken the American
model of an expensive, private club and used it here.
The clubhouse and surrounding grounds are
expansive and immaculate.

Built alongside a vast forested area, the eighteen
holes are arranged individually and separated from
each other by hilly landscapes that give each hole an
isolated feel. Although the water hazards are numerous, one can circumnavigate them fairly easily. The
long par threes are the backbone of the course, at
least visually. The eighth is a long par three at 240
yards that I parred with a driver and two putts. The
signature hole is the par three sixteenth with a lake on
the left and surrounding the left side of the green.
There are no short interesting par fours and one of
the par fives on each nine is a slog to hit the green in
regulation.

Golf Club Jakobsberg, Boppard/Rhens, Germany

Built in the mountains near Koblenz, Germany, this
course offers unmatched views of the Rhine Valley.
Jakobsberg was designed by Wolfgang Jersombek
and opened in 1992. The course is surrounded by
forest, mountains and ruins in the background, with
glimpses of the Rhine on almost every hole. The
Marksburg Castle is the aiming point of many of the
drives on this layout and confirms you are in Europe
playing golf. The tee markers are unusual as they are
shaped like Gummi Bears. Anyone who does not
have children or grandchildren probably doesn't know
about Gummi Bears, but they are the addictive candy

created in Germany in 1920. The current owner of
Jakobsberg is the CEO of the company which
produces them. Sweet!

I frankly do not remember much about the outgoing
nine other than that most of the holes were parallel,
back and forth, with two par fives and two par threes.
When that nine returned to the clubhouse, Bob
Rotella, the host for the cruise was waiting for our
foursome, which included Blake Griffith. Bob played
3-6 holes with every group during the trip and it was
our turn to have him play with us, a real treat! From
the first lecture or story Rotella told in the lectures he
gave each afternoon, he and Blake went back and
forth trying to one up each other. Blake would
interrupt Rotella's story with a comment or stupid
question etc. Well this was just a continuation of this
dialogue and fun for all. The three holes we played
with him were two interesting par fours, especially the
eleventh which bordered the only water hazard, and
the par five twelfth. It is a testimony to my concentration that I was able to make three bogeys with them
trading jabs at each other constantly.

Golf Club St. Leon-Rot, St. Leon-Rot, Germany

Just a few miles from the university town of
Heidelberg is St. Leon-Rot. It was designed by Dave
Thomas and completed in 2000. It has earned a high
profile as a rotating site of the Deutsche Bank SAP
Open. Woods won here in 1999, 2000 and 2002.
The City of Heidelberg is a fascinating old city and
worth the time for the 90 minute tour we took after
golf. It's home to the oldest university in Europe and
the majestic castle ruins of the Heidelberg Schlof.

On a 1977 visit here, I spent the whole day at this castle taking pictures while there was snow on the ground.

The course is situated in two paddocks, as the Australians would say, the first site containing the first and last holes. The second adjoining land has the outward nine rotating counter-clockwise around five small but scenic lakes. The long par four second and the 197 yard par three fourth are the most scenic. The huge undulating greens, well protected by nice bunkers, if one can call a bunker nice, are a treat in this layout in central Europe.

*Golf Club Soufflenheim Baden-Baden,
Souffenheim, France*

This club, 25 minutes from the French city of Strasbourg and 20 minutes from the world renowned spa of Baden-Baden, is located in the heart of the Alsace region of France and on the border with southern Germany. Designed by Bernhard Langer, it is composed of a short six hole course, another nine hole course and the championship course of 6,992 yards, reflecting the modern trend of "golf for everyone". Sofflenheim lies harmoniously within the water landscape of the upper Rhine valley surrounded by scenic views of the valley and dense forest.

The outgoing nine winds in a clockwise fashion among lakes on the outside of the property with the incoming nine inside the first, rotating counter-clockwise. Langer has created a good technical layout with water hazards and bunkering both being deterrents to a good score. The course is fairly flat with the fairways separated by numerous sandhills, giving each hole an isolated feeling.

Le Kempferhof Golf Club Strasbourg, France

Le Kempferhof Golf Club was created in 1989 in the Alsace region of Eastern France, on the German Border. The region is identified with Champagne, Ardenne and the Lorraine Vally and known locally as ACAL. The region has always been known for its hospitality and tradition. Yes! Really in France, the above adjectives are true. Kempferhof was designed by American Architect Robert Von Hagge who was inspired by the beauty of the landscape and the Rhine River. It has been ranked as high as fourth in the German Golf Journal and classified by Rolex Guide as one of the top fourteen courses in Europe.

Set on a secluded piece of land filled with beautiful pine, beech and birch trees, it is located 20 miles south of Strasbourg. The setting is enhanced by an old manor house that serves as the clubhouse. The routing is somewhat bizarre as it winds through the woods, ultimately ending with the ninth green situated on the left side of a huge horseshoe shaped green. The eighteenth occupies the right half of it. When we were there the two fairways were separated by a lake. Now, however, there is a huge elongated heart shaped bunker separating them. It is unusual, to say the least, but what can one say, but C'est La France n'est par? Nest ce pas?

I mentioned earlier that Dr. Bob Rotella was the host for the trip and every afternoon at tea or cocktail hour he would give us a very insightful lecture regarding golf psychology or his experiences with the various professionals whom he has coached. It was worth the cost of the trip to hear him talk and banter back and forth with Blake. Every night Bob and his adult daughter would sit at a different table, until he had dined with all the guests on the ship. The last night he sat with the Alders, Griffiths, Hughes, Faye and me. Well as we got ready to sit down, Rotella quipped: "Well, Blake if you had any hair and a big package (Blake is totally bald), you'd be hell on wheels." To which Susan Griffith came right back with: "one out of two ain't bad". Rotella was speechless for the first time in a week. Thus ended another great trip on an even higher or lower note.

I've ranked each course in the first three chapters. This chapter, however, deals with six courses in Portugal, and five courses spanning two countries in the Rhine River Valley. I feel it best to list each group separately since the two have little in common except that they are both in Western Europe; and I listed each separately after these two trips which were almost exactly ten years apart.

Algarve, Portugal

1. San Lorenzo Golf Club
2. Vale do Lobo (Royal Course)
3. Quinto do Largo (South Course)
4. Vila Sol Golf Club
5. Quinto do Largo (North Course)
6. Vilamoura I (Now Oceanico Old Course)

Rhine River Valley

1. Golf Club Gut Larchenhof
2. Jakobsberg Golf Club
3. Le Kempfehof Golf Club and Hotel
4. St. Leon-Rot Golf Club
5. Golf Club Soufflenheim

The two itineraries speak for themselves, so there is no reason to discuss what one should do. I do feel that if one wants to see Europe by boat or barge, it's probably better to leave the golf clubs at home.

Chapter V

The Caribbean Islands

Wikipedia defines The Caribbean Islands as "islands
that border or are surrounded by the Caribbean Sea".
There are twenty-five separate island nations; I have
only played golf on five of them, but have visited
others for sailing, on cruises and the beaches.   For
the sake of this discussion I'm including Bermuda in
this group, considerably north of the other islands, but
a convenient place to insert this island nation. (Figure
41)

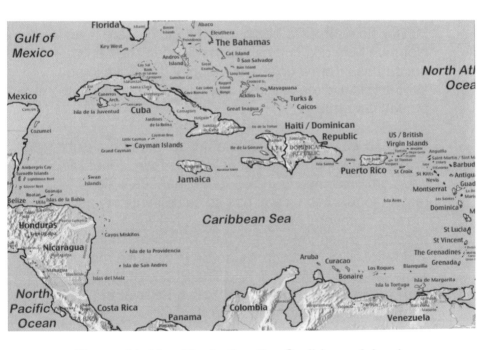

Figure 41. Map illustrating the Caribbean Islands

Part 1
Bermuda

The Mid Ocean Club, Tucker's Town, Bermuda

Mention golf in Bermuda and the first four words out of anyone's mouth are The Mid Ocean Club. The original development of this golf course started in 1913 when the Furness Withy Steamship company took an interest in developing a golf course to enhance tourism to the Island. Shortly thereafter Charles Blair McDonald, noted golf course architect, and Charles Wetmore, a structural architect, were hired to find a suitable site for the course and for a hotel. When the course was completed in 1921 McDonald wrote: "To begin with, I doubt if there is an eighteen hole golf course which will equal, certainly not surpass from a golfers standpoint, this links in any semi-tropical clime". Those words, until recently, have proven very true.

The Club was established as a private members club in 1951, and shortly thereafter Robert Trent Jones, Sr. was commissioned to make some changes which remain today. Mid Ocean has its place in history as the site of several summit meetings between President Eisenhower and Prime Ministers Churchill and MacMillan. President George H.W. Bush met with the Duke of Windsor and The Prince of Wales here as well. It has been host to two PGA Grand Slams of Golf in 2007 and 2008.

The contours of the course are unsurpassed, with valleys winding through coral hills from twenty to eighty feet in height. The fairways wind through wooded cedar trees, oleanders, bougainvillea and hibiscus plants which give the course a rainbow of color schemes. Faye and I came here for our twenty-fifth wedding anniversary in 1993, but I insisted on bringing my clubs and playing this course. If you go to Bermuda this is a "must do venue". I was a little late for my tee time with a caddie, you can never guess why, but I still remember the thrill of teeing off with a huge nautical flagpole to my left carrying the Union Jack, the Flag of Bermuda and the Mid Ocean Standard.

The first hole is a long, 400 yard par four sweeping down from an elevated tee adjacent to the club house, then back up to an elevated green. I remember being winded after hiking up the long hill to the elevated par three third. The fifth is the number one handicap, a par four, dogleg left around a lake, and is the signature hole on a layout with several lakes coming into play on the outgoing nine. The incoming nine's closing two holes are significant, with the par three seventeenth being a classic "Redan" design and the eighteenth a long uphill par four back up to the clubhouse. I've got it listed as seventy-seven in my list of favorites.

Turtle Hill Golf Club at
The Southhampton Princess

As mentioned, for our twenty-fifth anniversary we stayed at the Southampton Princess. The hotel remains the same with 500 plus rooms with every amenity one could ask for, but the name has changed to The Hamilton Princess Hotel & Beach Club. The golf course surrounding the property is an executive eighteen hole par three course. The views from high above the private pink sand beaches and vegetation

such as hibiscus and bougainvillea are spectacular. I
made the mistake of bringing my wife's clubs also.
She proved to me once and for all that a friend from
Montgomery's advice to not teach my wife to play golf
remains as good as gold.

Other courses of note in Bermuda are:
1. Tucker's Point Club, designed by Charles H.
Banks in 1932, it has recently been acquired by
Rosewood; they have significantly upgraded this
property.
2. The Port Royal Golf Club, designed by Robert
Trent Jones, Sr. in 1970, it has recently had a major
renovation directed by Robert Rulewich and looks
good in a recent magazine article. Another plus: this
course has also received significant funding by the
Bermudan Government.

Part II
The Bahamas

There are over 700 islands in the island nation of The
Bahamas, but only a few are big enough to support a
golf course allowing for both tourists and residents.
The northern most islands in the Bahama chain are
the Abacos, which are populated not only by Afro-
Americans, but also by English settlers who were
loyal to Great Britain during the American Revolution.
They fled America rather that give up their British
citizenship and were known as Loyalists in the
eighteenth century. I mentioned that other than golf,
blue water sailing has been another hobby of mine
and for that purpose my sail boat partner, John Swan,
and I sailed to the Bahamas in 2005. We ended up

mooring our boat at Hope Town on the Abaco island
of Elbow Cay.

The Abaco Islands

There are numerous islands in the Abacos. Marsh
Harbor on the island of Great Abaco is the largest city
in this chain. Grand Abaco Island, Elbow Cay,
Treasure Cay and Great Guana Cay are four of the
most prominent islands located here. Faye and I
spent New Year's and another week exploring every
cove and restaurant in this chain that is similar to the
British Virgin Islands with barrier islands protecting the
channel between the various islands.

Treasure Cay Golf Club at Treasure Cay Beach,
Marina & Golf Resort, Treasure Cay, Bahamas

Treasure Cay is a small island just north of Marsh
Harbor, located on the biggest island in the Abacos,
Grand Abaco. Until recently Treasure Cay Golf Club
was the only golf venue in the Abacos, as was the
case when Faye and I visited on one of our trips down
to our boat and the Abaco Islands in 2005. The
course opened for play in 1968 and was designed by
Dick Wilson. Wilson's style is designing elevated,
undulating greens, nicely framed with both bunkering
and foliage. The course measures 6,985 yards from
the tips and is a monster at that length. We sailed in
one afternoon, had a good dinner in the resort's
restaurant and I was ready to play in the morning.

The first tee is a minute cart ride from the marina and
I was so relaxed that I didn't realize I had played the
first two holes, a par four and a par five, in my
sandals. At that point I was even par and my two

playing companions didn't want me to change into the golf shoes in my bag. (Yes, I had taken a set of my clubs on the boat when we left Thanksgiving week from Destin, Florida.) It was an enjoyable round with a local boat mechanic and a fellow cruiser; the only difference was that he had a large fishing boat and I had a 35 foot sailboat.

The front nine has two scenic par threes with the only water on the outgoing nine being a small lake to the right of the short fourth at 145 yards from the regular tees. Probably the best hole is the par five eleventh, a dogleg right hole which bisects a lake. If the front nine is relatively devoid of water hazards the incoming nine makes up for it with water on seven of the nine holes. The eighteenth is a long par four, dogleg left, with a pond guarding the approach from the left side of the fairway. It makes for a good finishing hole.

Abaco's Other Courses

The other two top courses in the Abacos have been built since my visit in 2005. First is The Abaco Club @ Winding Bay in Marsh Harbor designed by Donald Steel and Tom Mackenzie. It is built on a beautiful stretch of beach and elevated coastline and developed by Peter de Savary who is known for his initial ownership of Skibo Castle. He has sold that recently, but retains similar properties in England, Rhode Island and South Carolina. You get to visit once to look things over and consider ownership.

Another property, Bakers Bay Club on Great Guana Cay, is a Discovery Land development with an eighteen hole Tom Fazio masterpiece. The last five holes allegedly rival Pebble Beach for dramatic ocean

views. You must be invited and accompanied by a
member to visit and play at this very private
development. Trust me I've unsuccessfully tried to
go. Although in 2016 Jordan Spieth, Ricky Fowler,
Justin Thomas and Smiley Kauffman had no trouble
booking condos there for their downtime after the
Masters.

Grand Bahama Island and Freeport

I've not played golf on Grand Bahama Island, which is
closer to Florida and just west of The Abacos. There
are three courses on this island. The Reef Course,
designed by Robert Trent Jones, Jr. in 2000, is an
eighteen hole contemporary links style course. The
Lucaya Course. located in Port Lucaya, has not had
very good reviews. Both of these courses are
associated with hotels: The Westin Hotel in Freeport
and The Sheraton in Lucaya. The third course is a
nine hole course in Freeport, Fortune Hills Golf and
Country Club. It was designed by Dick Wilson and
Joe Lee and has a very challenging third hole.

New Providence Island and Nassau

*Lyford Cay Club, Nassau, New Providence Island,
Bahamas*

Wade Hampton Golf Club has held an event termed
"The Safari" every winter to promote camaraderie,
and to let new members meet the established ones.
Beginning my first full year of membership in 1992,
we started the tradition of holding the Safari event at
Lyford Cay Club. Looking back on the fun times here,
it is hard to believe that Lyford was the host site until

2010. I had not heard of Lyford Cay previously, but realized it was located across New Providence Island from Nassau. The Safari was always held the first or second week in February and at a time when the weather, even in the south, was crummy. You got on the plane in Atlanta with rain or sleet and an hour and a half later landed in a place where you could exchange your corduroy slacks for Bermuda shorts. That is my kind of place! I should have known that I was in "high cotton" when I got the brochure quoting the room price at $550. I knew that was not enough for the four days, but in 1992 I had never paid that price for a room except in London or Paris. I called the head pro at Wade and ended up sharing a room, which was common then. That was before I started snoring.

The background on Lyford is interesting. It is a private, gated and guarded community located on the western tip of New Providence Island some 30 miles from Nassau and Paradise Island. It is named after Captain William Lyford, Jr., a mariner and British Loyalist who fought for the British in the American Revolution. As a reward for his services he received a land grant for 448 acres which ultimately became Lyford Cay Club. It remains one of the wealthiest and most exclusive developments in the world. The membership roster still reads like a 'who's who' in the world. There are several Greek shipping tycoons, the Bacardi family, and Henry Ford II's family to name a few. Sir John Templeton has a house overlooking the third fairway from a high bluff. I saw Sean Connery here on three separate occasions.

Wade Hampton always seemed to have a Lyford Cay member who was also a member to sponsor our

group. Our members flew down, frequently on the
same flight Sunday morning, played for four days and
came home on Thursday. Lyford basically turned the
club over to the 40-50 players who attended each
year. The regular members were barely inconvenien-
ced and their club benefited from a significant
amount of money infused. It was a winter paradise
with a few typical island glitches, the most
bothersome being the staff simply couldn't get our
orders or requests straight. Take dinner: one would
order a glass of wine and be billed for a bottle.
Frequently a table for four was charged a bottle of
wine apiece when at most we had imbibed two
bottles. On our recent visit here, that problem had
been solved. That fact notwithstanding, I know of no
golf resort where after eighteen holes you could come
in, have lunch, and then twenty to thirty people might
decide to play an emergency nine or captain's choice
and they could be accommodated so quickly. In short
it was the perfect venue for us.

It took me a couple of years to break the Bahamian
code in restaurants and bars. If you come in acting
rushed or in a hurry there is no way that you will get
your order in and get served in less than two hours. If
you come in acting like you have all the time in the
world, pulling out a book or magazine to read, you will
be served in no time. Trust me it works every time! I
probably took this trip 10-12 times so there are a
number of gambling, golf, and generally funny stories
about this trip. To be successful in gambling, golf and
eating a fast lunch, apparently you must be patient
and have staying power.

So here's a story or two. One of our gambling loving
members was down $25,000 at the baccarat table

and in a reversal won so much money before the night was over that he didn't have room in his golf bag to carry it all back home. And another. I've mentioned Blake Griffith before as being as bald as William McKee. Another night in the Paradise Island Casino, on the way out, he bet his last $100 chip and won on the blackjack table. His luck continued and he was playing 2-3 hands and winning thousands of dollars. William in the meantime was urging him to leave as we had a limousine waiting to take us back to Lyford; I was in the limousine when William told us about Blake. We got back to the table and a patron was telling his friend: " Listen I've never seen anything like this before. You've got this old man (probably 60 at the time) on a huge winning streak. Every time he wins $5,000 his son goes and cashes out and the dumb boy is begging him to leave the casino."

In 1994 or '95 I was in the last group on Wednesday, our last day of the tournament. Just as we were teeing off, three or four white limousines pulled up depositing ten or so Japanese men and women. (Nothing that unusual as we have all seen this scene before). On the green on number three, a long par four, we looked back and saw an army of golf carts, probably seven to eight, heading down the third fairway. Now the fourth tee is just left of the third green and three of the four Japanese players have hit their balls left of our tee in the palm trees but open enough to play. It was apparent at this point that these individuals were special as two carts contained women, two contained photographers and two contained security guards. One of the fellows in our group was having a bad start and was irritable as the Japanese players were running around and speaking loudly. One of us yelled fore and a couple of the

Japanese players stopped but one or two were still running around. I went to the very back of the tee, spread my arms out, and yelled 'fore GD' in my southern drawl. Well they all stopped in their tracks and didn't move. The closest one to me, some 20 yards away, was Prime Minister Morihiro Hosokawa of Japan coming over to a meeting with President Clinton in Washington. One of these days my bulldog mouth is going to get my chihuahua ass in trouble, but it didn't that day as the caddies and caddy master thought the scene was hilarious. Now to golf.

The Lyford Cay Golf Course was designed by Dick Wilson in the mid 1950's. It"s a par 72 layout in and out on each nine with a similar routing. The outward nine starts with a par five followed by a downhill par three. The holes in the middle of each nine are par fours except for the long par five fourth. The out-going nine ends with a long, dogleg par four. The incoming nine ends with the par three seventeenth over a pond and a long par five with multiple houses to the players' left.

In 2006 Rees Jones, with the help of Bruce Swanson, totally upgraded the course but didn't change the very good layout. It now has very fast greens of TifEagle bermuda that still have more grain than any other course I've ever played. A Wade Hampton group just returned to Lyford in February 2017 and nothing much has changed on this laid back, beautiful spot.(Figure 42) I must say a smaller group of the members of Wade Hampton told stories, made bets and had a great time on this outing which totally succeeded in its stated goal of camaraderie mentioned earlier.

Figure 42. The third hole at Lyford Cay Club with a typical cottage to the right

Other Courses in New Providence Island

1. *The One and Only Ocean Club Golf Resort* is associated with the mega family resort Atlantis. Anyone who has children and grandchildren should visit Atlantis as it has every water activity imaginable and is fun for all ages. The One and Only Ocean Club features 106 luxury rooms adjacent to the golf course. The course is on the eastern end of Paradise Island occupying land between the Atlantic Ocean and Nassau Harbor. As such I'm sure it has great views but I have not played it. It seems that on my recent two visits to Atlantis all of my time was taken up playing with my grandchildren and/or the course was being aerated.

2. *TPC Baha Mar at Laguna Beach* is a new resort
similar to Atlantis but catering more to adults. This
mega resort includes a new signature design golf
course by Jack Nicklaus. It was scheduled to open in
2016, but Nassau being Nassau the opening is still
delayed as of 2017. Originally Cable Beach Golf
Course, is being completely redesigned for this
venue.

3. Three years ago while visiting my family in Augusta
I asked a friend where his daughter and son-in-law
were. He replied that they were spending New Year's
in Albany. I thought, then vocalized, "Why in the world
would anyone spend New Year's in Albany, Georgia?"
I was quickly corrected. They were in the Bahamas
visiting friends at *Albany Golf Club* on the southern
side of New Providence Island, a new ultra exclusive
resort frequented by golf pros and the ultra wealthy.
The Ernie Els design, 7,400 yard course, combines
links with windswept dunes and desert landscapes.
Homes start at five million and the rate per night is
$2,500. I also understand that the course is very hard.

Great Exuma Island

Grand Isle Resort and Spa has an eighteen hole
championship golf course designed by Greg Norman
on Great Exuma Island. There are a series of
dramatic holes winding through the dunes, with six
holes hugging Emerald Bay's scenic peninsula. The
final holes are set on yet another rocky peninsula that
offers high views of the crashing ocean below.

Eleuthera Island

In the mid 1990's a member of Wade Hampton, Buddy Rice, invited several groups of his friends to come down to Eleuthera to visit, as he and his wife had just bought a lovely house on the island. I can't remember ever being as relaxed as I was on that trip. We played The Cotton Bay Golf Course which in the 1950's and 1960's was a prominent vacation spot. The course was designed by Robert Trent Jones, Sr., but by the 1990's it was in rough shape. The grass was long, greens unkept, and the golf carts had been cannibalized to keep two or three running. My understanding is that the course has basically gone to grass with no upkeep and some holes missing pins. It is very sad to see this happen to any beautiful and enjoyable spot in the world.

Part III
Cuba

Yes. I've played golf on the only maintained golf course in Cuba, Varadero Golf Club in the seaside resort of Varadero. In 2001 my sailboat partner, John Swan and I got permission to sail to Cuba, enter and dock at the Hemingway Marina, which has been the marine destination in Havana for hundreds of years. After arrival we were bombarded with approximately 18 officials from customs officials, and agricultural inspectors to physicians, inspecting our boat. All wanted treats from Oreo cookies and cokes to beer and rum. The Cubans love sweets and alcohol as they take some coffee with their sugar.

Having cleared that hurdle of checking in, we were met by a man whose job it was to act as our tour guide and Boy Friday. After helping us tie up in a parallel slip in Hemingway Marina, (Figure 43) he siphoned some gas from one car to his friend's Russian Lada and obtained enough gas to get the car to a service station. We then bought gas to drive the ten miles into Old Havana. You cannot make up stories like these. Five of us were packed into the car

Figure 43. "SV Morning Star" docked in the parallel slip in Hemingway Marina

like sardines in a can, the car not being anymore substantial than a sardine can.

Going to Old Havana is like stepping into a time machine and being transported to New Orleans of the 1940's and 1950's. The buildings are magnificent but crumbling from lack of care. It's a real shame that on subsequent visits nothing has yet changed. The restaurant all the yachting magazines recommended was La Gallega, housed on the third floor of a huge old house in Old Town Havana. The food was excellent and cheap with wonderful service. The only drawback: the house looked like it might crumble to the ground at any time and all floors were taken up with small crowded apartments.

The Miramar neighborhood in Havana, where the city's wealthy moved, and the location of most of the embassies, is still beautiful and not as rundown as the rest of the city. A British diplomat years ago built a nine hole course for the diplomats to play. We looked for it, but understand that basically it has "gone to grass". Apparently the layout is intact but the greens are awful and the holes are marked by tree branches. We looked for it again on our sailing trip here in 2003 but couldn't find it.

Varadero Golf Club, Varadero, Matanzas Provdenc, Cuba

The original course here was the nine hole private course (circa 1936) of Irenee du Pont who owned the beach side property along with the family mansion, Xanadu. In the early 1990's Castro, apparently recognizing the value of tourism, hired Les Furber, a former Trent Jones associate, to lengthen the course to eighteen holes. After visiting in 2001, my zany new goal was to build a high end golf club in Cuba; to that end I asked the developer of Wade Hampton, William McKee, to accompany me to Cuba before our 'safari trip' in 2002. We flew to Nassau, changed planes and flew to Havana taking our golf clubs with us.

With the same guide as in 2001, on our third day in Havana, we headed east to Varadero and checked in to the Melia Las American Hotel. The Melia Hotels, a Spanish chain, are the best bet for hotels in Cuba. After a good seafood meal at the hotel's restaurant, the next morning we set out for a round at Varadero. The first twelve holes are straight forward back and forth with parallel fairways several hundred yards from the ocean with two high rise hotels dominating the landscape. These holes were flat with wide landing areas and well bunkered greens which were slow. It reminds me of any generic south Florida course with palm, mangrove and almacigo trees lining the fairway.

On the other hand, the incoming nine is interspersed with flower fringed salt inlets and the last six holes are unique and beautiful. Pedro (Chubby) Klein, the overseer and administrator of Varadero, says that thirteen through eighteen make the journey from Havana worthwhile. The tee shot at thirteen plays to an angled, elevated plateau that drops off left over a coral outcropping. The fourteenth, dogleg right, offers one a short cut, but risks one having a lost ball or unplayable lie. Fifteen, a long par four, has a long forced carry over a pretty inlet to a narrow green. Sixteen is another long par five that crosses over water twice, but the carries are not as severe as fifteen. Seventeen is a 200 yard par three that plays longer because of the elevated, bunker fringe green. The eighteenth is definitely the signature hole, as it runs along a high bluff with the ocean on the left and the green hugging the edge. (Figures 44 & 45).

Figure 44. Varadero's eighteenth looking west with the Caribbean Sea in the background

Figure 45. Valadaro's eighteenth looking east with the clubhouse and Xanadu mansion on the right

On my first visit to Cuba in 2001, we traveled fifty miles west of Havana to get a feel for the countryside. Instead of beaches, there is a mountain range with elevations up to 3,500 feet with beautiful scenery and waterfalls. The foliage is dense but the long range views of mountains and the ocean are wonderful. I thought then that this location would make a wonderful site for a golf course. With that plan in mind I had made an appointment with Chubby Klein. William and I had a long talk with him after our round. He was very affable, spoke fluent English and very receptive to building another course in Cuba. William felt that there was not enough infrastructure to do what I wanted do, not to mention that one cannot get a clear title to any of the land here.

Part IV
Jamaica

I do not think anyone should go to Jamaica for golf, but if you go for the beach, laid back atmosphere and the weather, there are several good courses to try. I will describe the only course I've played here. It was associated with the hotel I was staying in for an ENT meeting in the late 1990's. There are several better known ones around Montego Bay on the northern shore of this island just south of Cuba, but I haven't seen them.

Runaway Bay Golf Course, Runaway Bay Jamaica, West Indies

Built in 1960 by a British Naval Commander, John Harris, Runaway Bay is heralded as one of the best courses in Jamaica. It has hosted numerous Jamaican Opens as well as a World Cup Qualifier. Its location is good: east of Montego Bay on the northern coast of the island. The course is mainly an up and back par 72 with the usual four par threes, four par fives, and you guessed it, ten par fours. There are memorable elevation changes for a course so close to sea level, but the conditioning was not good and the greens slow. The reasonably good caddies were trying to convince my foursome of physicians that we were playing the best layout in Jamaica, although further research has proven otherwise, as I will recount below.

There are a handful of good and apparently interesting courses both east and west of Montego Bay; probably the most famous is The White Witch Golf Course at Rose Hall again, east, of Montego Bay. Designed by Robert von Hagge in 2000, and associated now with the Hyatt Zilara Rose Hall Hotel, formally the Ritz-Carlton. The course intertwines with the mountains and provides one with great views of the sea from higher elevations. Half Moon Golf Club associated with The Half Moon Resort adjacent to the Hyatt east of the city is another good course designed by Robert Trent Jones, Sr.

Tryall Club, Jamaica, located thirty miles west of Montego Bay is probably the best course in Jamaica. Designed by Ralph Plummer in 1960, this exclusive golf resort opened three years later on a seventeenth century sugar plantation and is the most manicured course on the island. When Faye and I visited Negril in the winter of 2015, as I was recovering from major back surgery, we drove through this resort. Based on what I saw, if I go back, this is where I will stay and play.

Part V
Dominican Republic

The Dominican Republic Island attached to Haiti on its western border, has slowly and enterprisingly converted itself into a "must do" site for any traveling golfer. The courses here are convenient to travel to, especially from the east coast, and rival the venues in Mexico or Hawaii for beauty, sea vistas and originality. This all started in 1971 when Pete Dye designed Casa de Campo, "Teeth of the Dog" Golf Course, and the resort of that name was developed. The second transforming event occurred when the Punta Cana International Airport was built as the first privately owned airport in the world in 1984. It services the south east side of the island and gives access to numerous beach resorts, casinos and the Cap Cana Resort as well as the Punta Cana Resort, both of which have top end seaside courses as we will discuss. PUJ is now the second busiest airport in the Caribbean.

From the mid 1970's, when Casa de Campo was written up in numerous golf journals, I knew it was only a matter of time until I traveled to this course. In 2007 my friend, Jay Johnston, an attorney in Birmingham, AL, and I made plans to go in November when Wade Hampton closed. Another member of WH advised that if we were going to the Dominican Republic we had to play Punta Espada, the new Jack Nicklaus course at the Cap Cana Resort.

Well to make a long story short, we stayed in a Paradisus Resort in Punta Cana and went over to Casa de Campo the first day. The second day we played Punta Espada and found the conditioning as good as advertised and were so impressed with it that we went back and played it again on the day we left. After having won the bets the first two days, Jay beat the socks off me the third day. Had he not won, that last day, he would have probably died down there and it would have been hell to pay getting his body shipped home. This was the second golf trip that Jay and I took together and after returning, I told his wife Marjorie, that it would be the last trip I intended to take with Jay. It seems that he was such a bad influence on me at meals, I had gained five pounds on two four day trips with him and had to go a diet.

Casa de Campo, Teeth of the Dog, La Romana, Dominican Republic

East of Santo Domingo, between the capital and Punta Cana, this resort is located in La Romana, a medium sized city, that before a four lane motorway was built, was a terrible hassle to travel through. In 2007 it took us over three hours to travel to Casa de Campo from Punta Cana. Now it takes less than an hour. The course gets its name from the craggy, irregular, rocky shoreline that looks similar to dogs' teeth. The course starts out winding through towering bluffs before coming out on the Caribbean Sea at the fifth hole. This is a dramatic sea hugging par three signature hole which is guarded by a lone tree that one must negotiate over or around. The sixth, seventh and eighth run along the beach before turning inland. The ninth through the thirteenth are more reminiscent of a parkland layout, but the dramatic finish includes three holes above the rocks. It is definitely worth driving over one day from Punta Cana now that one no longer suffers through the arduous conditions of 2007. I have it ranked 107 in my list of favorites.

The other two courses at Casa de Campo are the older, Links Course, similar to the more traditional links in the UK, winding through the interior of the resort with occasional views of the ocean and the dramatic Dye Fore Course. Both of these courses were designed by Pete Dye, but the photographs of the new Dye Fore are dramatic as the course is built on a high ridge overlooking the Chavon River, the Altos de Chavon and the resort's marina.

The Cap Cana Resort, Punta Espada Course

The Cap Cana Resort property began development in the early 2000's as an optimistic, mega resort of over 9,000 acres. The resort had projections for five golf courses: three designed by Jack Nicklaus, one developed by Donald Trump and the fifth by another prominent golf course architect. The downturn in 2008 hit this planning hard. To date only one of the signature Nicklaus courses has been built but if the quantity of planned courses is less than hoped for, the quality of Punta Espada leaves absolutely nothing to be desired.

Built in 2006 on the south-eastern tip of the Dominican Republic (Figure 46), this course is a magnificent layout with beautiful vistas of the Caribbean Sea at every turn. It has been voted the best course in the Caribbean and Mexico by "GolfWeek Magazine", and has hosted The Cap Cana Championship, a PGA Champions Tour Event, from 2008-2010. Fred Couples won the event in 2010 by shooting a 62 in the final round. Having played this course five times, that score is truly amazing to me.

Figure 46. The Southern Tip of The DR with the two resorts illustrated

Figure 47. The front of Punta Espada's second green with the inlets and the seventeenth hole in the background

The course starts out with the back tees perched high on a rock outcropping on a long par four. The second is a dogleg right par five that incorporates an inlet which drains into the Caribbean Sea. (Figure 47) The third runs down the seacoast with the ocean on the right and the fourth is a long par three with an ocean inlet as an imposing hazard. The remaining holes on the outgoing nine are slightly inland with an abundance of sandy waste areas that eventually end back at the clubhouse.

The tenth is a sweeping dogleg right with a lake to the right of the fairway and green. The layout comes back to the ocean on the par five twelfth and the thirteenth, which is a dramatic par three similar to Cypress' sixteenth, except as a mirror image. (Figure 48)

Nicklaus's design incorporates the natural features of the landscape into the course's topography, the bluffs, the beach, the water and the foliage, probably better than any of his other courses. Fittingly the course finishes along the rocky coastline on the golfer's right with two magnificent par fours the seventeenth and the eighteenth. I have Punta Espada rated fifty-fifth (55) in my list of favorites.

There are three ranges of accommodations at Cape Cana. First, The Eden Roc, a Relais & Chateaux high end property right on the beach and adjacent to the incoming nine holes here. Next are the Alsol Tiara Suites and Condominiums, designed with families and golf buddy trips in mind. Lastly, there is The Sanctuary Hotel which has a Spanish motif; it is also quite nice

Figure 48. Punta Espada's signature thirteenth hole

The Punta Cana Resort & Club, Corales Golf Club

The Corales Golf Club is the headliner course in the other golf resort in the south-east corner of the Dominican Republic. My advice when planning a trip here: book directly with The Westin Hotel at Punta Cana. When I came back here in 2012 with my good friends Mid Parker and Clifford Johnston, the Punta Cana Resort absolutely could get nothing right. I spent untold hours trying to get the tee times, restaurant reservations and all arrangements correct. If it hadn't been for Jay Overton, the Manager and Head Pro at Corales, it never would have happened. As an illustration of this fact I will recall for you the aberration of ordering drinks. The Punta Cana Resort is an all inclusive one - alcohol is included. Mid Parker does not imbibe, drinks only CocaCola which they charged him for each time. After all the mishaps, miscues and generally hard times with bookings, the resort understood my constant complaints. When Mid was checking out, he saw his large CocaCola bill, said he understood, but the desk clerk allowed as when you're with Dr. Kitchens there is no charge.

Nevertheless, this course is wonderful with ocean scenery similar to Punta Espada, great greens and a more forgiving layout. Tom Fazio designed this course in 2010 along the natural cliffs, bays, inland lakes and beautiful ocean coves. The course starts out in a clockwise rotation toward the north. The first six holes are slightly inland with lots of sand and lakes. (Figure 49)

Figure 49. The back corner of Corales' second hole with the third hole in the background

The inward nine begins toward the south in a counter-clockwise direction, winding around mounds, natural foliage and coralina quarries. The fourteenth is a 626 yard monster from the Championship tees and the course measures 7,650 yards from those tees. However, from the senior tees the course is much more manageable at 5,926 yards. I like every Fazio course I've ever played, primarily because most of his courses are hard but not unfairly so. He doesn't try to trick the golfer: what you see is what you get; good shots get rewarded and bad shots get penalized.

This is very true on Corales' layout as it crescendos to the last three holes nicknamed "The Devil's Elbow", because the par five eighteenth demands an accurate tee shot to a narrow peninsula fairway that juts out into the Caribbean Sea. This is a very impressive setting with the waves crashing into the coral and rocks surrounding this peninsula. (Figure 50)

Figure 50. Corales' dramatic eighteenth set on a peninsula jutting out into the Caribbean Sea: "The Devil's Elbow"

The preceding two holes run up to the ocean, also giving the golfer more dramatic views of the coastline.

Mid Parker and I liked the trip to the Dominican Republic so much that when a fellow member of Wade Hampton, who has a condo in Cap Cana, asked us if we wanted to go down again, we promptly accepted his offer. Never give Mid and me an invitation for a golf trip unless you really want us to come. So, Mid and I invited two other Wade golfing buddies, Morgan Fayssoux, whom I've written about previously, and another close friend, Taliaferro Lane.

We played both Punta Espada and Corales twice. On the last night we had the best meal of the trip at a top ranked steak place. I had an uncomfortable night with generalized abdominal pain, nausea etc. Despite this, I was determined to play Corales one more time. Well when the other three guys went for breakfast, which I never miss, I remained lying on the back seat of our SUV, nauseated. My sickness continued and as they were warming up, I was still lying on a couch in the small, delightful pro shop and grill, drinking club soda with lime. I jumped up ten minutes later and, you know what? I played my best round of the trip, winning all bets. The moral of this story is beware the sick golfer!!

I have Corales ranked sixty-six (66) in my list of favorites, and I'm sure you will enjoy these two courses in the Dominican Republic.

The choices for lodging here are The Westin at Punta Cana and the high end Tortuga Bay which was the only AAA rated hotel in the Dominican Republic in

2014. Tortuga Bay is located right on the beach at The Punta Cana Resort.

The Punta Cana Resort & Club, La Cana Golf Club

The other golf course at Punta Cana Resort is P. B. Dye's La Cana Course. This 27 hole complex is adjacent to The Punta Cana Resort's bungalows. Unfortunately, in 2012, because of the death of my friend Blake Griffith, I missed seeing the original eighteen hole layout here. The original two nines are named Tortuga and Arrecife and fourteen of the eighteen holes have ocean views. Mid Parker and Clifford Johnston found the conditioning not up to the other courses' standards, but it is hard to beat the other courses discussed here. I did, however, play the new Hacienda nine later in 2012 and thought it was a great inland, tropical layout in immaculate condition.

Part VI
St. Maarten

Faye and I went to the island St. Maarten on the Dutch side of the island, or St. Martin for the French side, in the late 1990's for a winter vacation and ENT medical seminar. The island is a nice place to visit in the winter for sun, surf and sand. I love the beach and to sit under an umbrella and watch the people, mainly the ladies, go by. The Orient Beach, on the French side, is a nude beach. Although I went, I didn't obey the nude part of the clothing optional beach. I found that the girls you wanted to see nude were not and the ones that you could care less to see were!

Mullet Bay Golf Club, Mullet Bay, St. Maarten

I was warned that a hurricane devastated the island and this golf course in 1995, but I was determined to lug my clubs down and play this course. You probably know that mullet is a common, plentiful fish that smells to high heaven. I found out quickly that this course was appropriately named. Designed by Joe Lee in 1990, until the hurricane passed through, it probably was good. The layout had some elevation changes and the incoming nine had two holes on Mullet Bay, but the par 70 course was in rough condition, and the partially built, partially destroyed buildings of the Mullet Bay Resort made things much worse. I did have a nice caddy but understand that amenity is no longer available. We went back to start a Star Clipper Sailing Cruise (2015) and rode by the course on the way to the airport and found it to be open but still in poor shape.

Ranking of the twelve courses I have played in the Caribbean Islands

1. Punta Espada at Cap Cana Resort, DR, #55
2. Corales Golf Club at Punta Cana Resort, DR, #66
3. The Mid Ocean Club, BM, #77
4. Casa de Campo, DR, #107
5. Lyford Cay Club, New Providence, Bahamas
6. Varadero Golf Club, Cuba
7. Treasure Cay Golf Club, Treasure Cay, Bahamas
8. La Cana Golf Club, DR
9. Runaway Bay Golf Club, Jamaica
10. Turtle Hill Golf Club at Fairmont Southampton, BM
11. Cotton Bay Golf Club, Eleuthera, Bahamas
12. Mullet Bay Golf Club, St. Maarten

As far as presenting a sample itinerary for the Caribbean, the only island that warrants an exclusive visit for golf is the Dominican Republic. So on a trip to the Dominican Republic, I would fly down to Punta Cana International Airport, stay in either the Punta Cana Resort or the Cap Cana Resort. Play twice at Punta Espada and twice at Corales at the Punta Cana Resort. Whichever resort you stay in, the golf is slightly discounted, but at the other it's inflated. It's almost worth while to stay two nights in each one. Play once at the La Cana Golf Club in the Punta Cana Resort as well, but insist on playing the Hacienda nine.

I would then travel over to Casa de Campo and play it along with the Dye Fore course; it sounds interesting, as it is set in the high river bluffs. That would be seven courses in seven days, easily doable without much strain. You can easily rent a car for the trips back and forth to the various resorts.

Chapter VI

Mexico

To get to Mexico's courses one must fly across the Gulf of Mexico, the Sea of Cortez or the Pacific Ocean from the United States. So technically you are crossing a pond to play here. I could just as easily have titled this chapter 'Los Cabos' because, with one exception, I've only played courses in this region on the tip of Mexico's Baja peninsula. The district, or county of Los Cabos, is an area comprising half of the Baja California Sur peninsula below La Paz, the capital city. The area includes two cities, San Jose del Cabo, on the east side and Cabo San Lucas on the western tip of the Baja. (Figure 51) First dis-covered for its deep sea fishing, Cabo San Lucas became known as the Marlin Capital of the World. Today the area is heralded as Mexico's number one golf resort destination and I certainly agree with that assessment. The tip of Cabo San Lucas, best known for its rock formation, "El Arco", is where the Pacific Ocean joins the Sea of Cortez.

In 1990 a successful California developer and avid golfer, Don Koll, commissioned Jack Nicklaus to design and build twenty-seven holes of golf for his resort Palmilla, now known as The One & Only Palmilla Resort and Golf Club. In the 26 years follow-ing this development, Los Cabos has become a world class golfing mecca which features no less that twelve major courses designed by some of the best known golf architects in the world. I won't say that this destination is as good as Hawaii, but it's one helluva lot closer to the continental United States and the courses here rival anything in Hawaii.

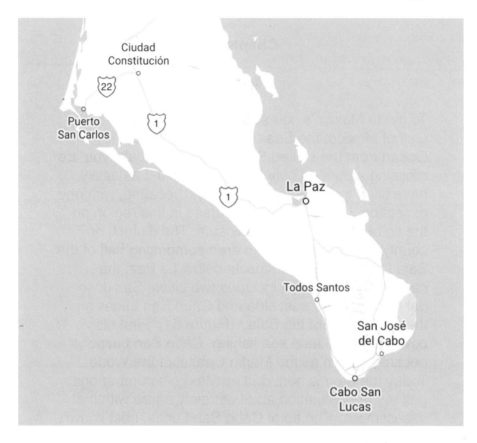

Figure 51. Map of the lower half of The Baja
Peninsula

In 1998, our Wade Hampton group of sixteen, including wives, known as the Rendezvous group, decided
to come here for our sixth golfing trip together. Little
did we know that this would be our last trip together
for many reasons. We chose the Palmilla Resort for
lodging. The atmosphere and service were great on
this and on a subsequent visit two years later. (Figure
52) I haven't visited Los Cabos since January 2014,
but understand that the hurricane later that year devastated everything on the beach. The rebuilding has

changed most all of the properties, all for the best.

Figure 52. Palmilla's infinity pool with rocky beach and Sea of Cortez in background

Palmilla Golf Club, San Jose del Cabo, Baja California Sur, Mexico

This award winning course, on the eastern side of what is known as the Tourist Corridor between San Jose del Cabo and Cabo San Lucas, is composed of three nine hole tracts. It is currently managed by Troon Golf and as mentioned, designed by Jack Nicklaus. The first two nine holes, Arroyo and Mountain were designed first, with the Ocean nine opening shortly before our visit in 1998. The Mountain nine was my favorite starting out with three long par fours, the third an uphill 470 yard brute which has been mentioned as one of the greatest par fours in the world. The fourth, a par five, is sandwiched between two lakes and the fifth is probably my favorite hole at Palmilla. It's a long par four with a forced carry across a canyon with scrub to a landing area that requires a second shot to carry yet another narrow version of this canyon to an isolated green.

The Arroyo nine is routed through the deep canyons and measures 3,337 from the tips. The first three are par fours, all dogleg right, and the dramatic fourth runs between two lakes, the first of which is shared with the par three sixth on the Mountain nine. The fifth, sixth and seventh are probably the most visually dramatic in Palmilla as they all present high, long range views of the Sea of Cortez.

The newest nine holes, the Ocean nine, measures 3,527 yards from the back and has a 600 foot drop in elevation from the clubhouse to the ocean. The third comes down to the Sea of Cortez with the green essentially on the beach. After a high, short par three in the sand, the fifth returns to the ocean and the picture perfect par three sixth on the beach is the only hole that the Kitchens family birdied on this course. That was accomplished by my novice wife with two wonderful shots.

Cabo del Sol Golf, (Ocean Course), Cabo San Lucas, Baja California Sur, Mexico

I consider this Jack Nicklaus course his finest work and the "Must Play" course in Mexico. It's located almost exactly half way between Cabo San Lucas and San Jose del Cabo. Nicklaus has been quoted as saying Cabo del Sol has the "three best finishing holes in the world." All are located on the rocky cliffs above the Sea of Cortez almost in sight of "El Arco".

The Ocean Course occupies 1.5 miles of cliff hanging beachfront property that has been touted as the best piece of golf property in the world. It has been ranked in the top 100 courses in the world by Golf Magazine and has been called "The Pebble Beach of Mexico."

The outgoing nine rotates in a clockwise direction with a straight away par four followed by a dogleg right one and a short par four measuring 327 yards from the tips. The par five fourth turns south toward the ocean and the fifth goes down to the beach, the former affording great long range views of the Sea of Cortez, and the latter close views of the beautiful beach. The sixth and seventh, both par threes, run parallel to the ocean and jut out on a small peninsula. The eighth goes back up from the shore and the ninth runs parallel to the first hole.

The incoming nine rotates in a counterclockwise direction weaving back and forth in the sand dunes and scrub brush. The par five fifteenth, similar to number four, affords one a long and high distance view of the ocean, while the sixteenth again runs down to the ocean and is obviously the start to the famous closing holes. (Figure 52)

The seventeenth is a 178 yard par three which demands a precise shot over a sandy beach and rock outcroppings to a small green with bunkers on the right and a long drop to the churning ocean below. The eighteenth, with rock cliffs falling to the ocean on

Figure 52. Cabo del Sol's par five fifteenth with the
Sea of Cortez in background

the left, was modeled after the eighteenth at Pebble
Beach except it's a mirror image. I have Cabo del Sol
ranked sixty-second in my list of favorites.

*Cabo del Sol (Desert Course), Cabo San Lucas, Baja
California Sur, Mexico*

The Desert course, designed by Tom Weiskopf,
incorporates the natural beauty of the desert. It had
not been constructed on our first trip to Los Cabos
and I have chosen not to play it on subsequent visits.

*Cabo Real Golf Club, San Jose del Cabo, Baja
California Sur, Mexico*

One of the first courses in Los Cabos not designed by
Nicklaus, Cabo Real, was designed by R.T. Jones Jr.
in 1994. The outgoing nine, refashioned by Jones
from a pre-existing layout, is a somewhat forgiving
design with broad fairways running down to the Sea
of Cortez. There are three ocean front holes, then a
short par four fifth plays across an arroyo en route to
the beach. The par three sixth hole is located on a

sea side bluff which gives the golfer a beautiful view of the beach framed by palm trees.

With holes chiseled into the desert foothills adjacent to the mountains, the incoming nine is more of a target golf course. The seventeenth is a long par four, right to left dogleg that has two large fairway bunkers, a lone cactus and a small green situated into a hill. The closing par five eighteenth has a forced carry over an arroyo on the right and a lake on the left. In short, I was not that impressed with the layout and the required "target golf" shots.

Eldorado or El Dorado Golf Club, Cabo San Lucas, Baja California Sur, Mexico

Initially this course, a Jack Nicklaus signature design, was part of the Cabo Real Resort. Accompanied by two other members of Wade Hampton, I played this course when we returned for a visit in 2000. Since then Discovery Land acquired the property and turned it into a private club similar to all of the Discovery Land Properties; therefore, if you do not know a member of a Discovery Land complex you are out of luck. I furthermore understand that Discovery took three of the most dramatic ocean front holes and turned them into home sites. The initial club name was Eldorado, but now it is known as El Dorado.

As the signature designation suggests, Nicklaus apparently spent hours walking the rugged coastline, the quiet desert and shaded canyons of this great site before designing a tract that blends with the natural landscapes described above. The outgoing nine is unusual in that it has three par threes, three par fours and three par fives. I was very fortunate to play the course before two of the most beautiful ocean holes I have ever played were redesigned. I believe these were the eleventh, a dogleg left par four sweeping down to a green on the beach, and the thirteenth, an even more dramatic par five also rotating counter - clockwise giving one an even better view of the Sea of Cortez. I probably listed it among my favorites early on, but since they've changed it, I hesitate to have it on my list.

Querencia Golf Club

This course and residential development is without question the best course and private residential development in Los Cabos; for that matter in all Mexico and the Caribbean. Designed by Tom Fazio as his first course outside of the United States in 1999, it is a joy to see and experience playing it. As one is driving in from the primary road linking San Jose del Cabo and Cabo San Lucas you can feel the understated elegance of this community and its accompanying golf course. I think the one thing that stood out in my mind as I played Querencia is that every hole has specular views of western San Jose del Cabo, the Sea of Cortez and the desert landscape. (Figure 53) Each hole seems somewhat isolated from its neighbor, yet the routing flows down toward the Sea of Cortez without ever reaching it. The views in all directions are stunning panoramas from the high plateaus with the holes winding through desert and deep arroyos to the ever present ocean scenes.

The outgoing nine starts out at the apex of the property and literally tumbles down southward toward the Sea of Cortez. The first and third holes are relatively short par fours interspersed with the long par three second.

Figure 53. Querencia's fourth and fifth holes looking east toward San Jose del Cabo

The fourth, a 500+ yard par five, which because of its tight fairway, has the number one handicap rating, is followed by a short but narrow par four with the number three handicap. The remaining holes on the outward nine fall south toward the ocean, with the ninth, a long par five, being the southern most point of the course. (Figure 54)

The incoming nine turns back north, but not before one has an opportunity to have some refreshments in the Oasis Bar. The holes here blend seamlessly into the desert landscape with contoured fairways, greens

Figure 54. Querencia's par five ninth hole with the
Sea of Cortez in the background

with subtle breaks and oddly shaped beautiful
bunkers. My friend Mid Parker, previously mentioned,
feels like Querencia has the most difficult greens to
putt. As testimony to that end, I three putted three of
the first four holes, but once I started taking the
caddie's advice, they ran very true when you knew
where to hit the putts.

The greens and fairways blend into the native foliage
in a wonderful way and make this tract very
appealing. To that end, "Golfweek" magazine rates
Querencia number one in Mexico and I agree with
that rank completely. In my list of favorites I have it
fifty-two, the highest rated course south of the border.

Diamante Golf Club (Dunes Course)

Until recently this course was the only Los Cabos course located on the Pacific Ocean. Designed by Davis Love III in 2008, it opened in 2009 and promptly received the honor of being named the Top New International Golf Course in 2010 by "Golf Magazine". This publication continues to rank it higher than other golf magazines, having ranked it 38th in the world most recently in 2015. In 2012 "Golf Digest" rated the Dunes Course the number one course in Mexico. The eighteen hole layout is stretched along one of the most pristine beaches anywhere on the Pacific Ocean and offers the most dramatic sand dunes this side of Carne Golf Club in Ireland.

This is David Love III's twentieth course design and easily his best work. He has stated: "You're either playing toward the ocean, along the ocean or away from the ocean". The tips measure out at 7,300 yards, with the outgoing nine 700 yards shorter than the incoming nine. This is due to the fact that there are three par threes on the outgoing nine which circles in a roughly clockwise direction and ends back at the clubhouse. Par is 35-37, primarily because there are three par fives on the incoming side which also rotates in a clockwise direction south of the clubhouse.

The layout, one of the true links in the Western Hemisphere, begins with a medium length par five to the north. All of the cart paths are well placed railroad ties which are certainly more esthetically pleasing than asphalt or concrete. The second is a long, downhill par three that ends in a natural bowl green set between the dunes. The third and fourth are both medium length, slightly dogleg par fours routed between the dunes enroute to the beach The fifth is a classic uphill par three with the Pacific as a backdrop. (Figure 55)

Figure 55. Diamante's fifth, an uphill par three headed toward The Pacific Ocean

The remainder of the outgoing nine rotates away from the ocean on the western periphery of the course. The holes include a par five that runs along the beach into the prevailing wind, another par three and two par fours. The ninth is set into a grove of cardon cacti with a forced carry across an arroyo to reach the green.

Turning to the incoming nine from the clubhouse, one encounters a downwind drive from an elevated tee to the longest par four on the course. Another uphill par three follows and heads out for the only two holes not set by the ocean. When I visited in the winter of 2014 they were already eliminating these two holes in favor of two more along the ocean to keep the course's dunes theme. I believe the par four fifteenth is the truest links-like hole on the course, with the green set at the base of a very high dune protecting the green from the ocean. (Figure 56)

Figure 56. Diamante's fifteenth hole with the Pacific Ocean in the background

The sixteenth is a lovely par three directly into the prevailing wind and setting sun with the beach and ocean as a backdrop. The par five seventeenth sports the world's largest sand bunker with the beach coming into play. The eighteenth is a demanding, uphill par four that requires a forced carry over an arroyo to give one a chance to reach the green in regulation. Overall, it's a great design on an unbelievable beach front setting and I have it listed eighth-five in my list of favorites.

Diamante Golf Club (El Cardonal Course)

When I visited Diamante in January of 2014 this course had been graded and shaped and the grass was just being planted. This is Tiger Woods' creation in Los Cabos where he was working with my friend Beau Welling. It's Tiger's second completed work, as it opened in mid December 2014. Set back from the coast among mature vegetation, sand dunes and natural arroyos, in contrast to the earlier Dunes Course it has long range views of the Pacific Ocean.

Other courses in Los Cabos

1. Chileno Bay Golf and Beach Club is Tom Fazio's latest design in Cabo San Lucas. The course opened in late December of 2013, but had a somewhat slow start until Discovery Land Company acquired the property in 2015. Its location is excellent being ten miles west of another Discovery project, El Dorado. Discovery used the same model as with El Dorado i.e., took an existing development, privatized it and redeveloped it as a private club. The course is rumored to be spectacular with the practice range and holes facing the Sea of Cortez, and two holes bringing Lake Chileno into play. An exclusive VieVage Hotel opened in the fall of 2016 and allows guests to have access to an otherwise private club.
2. Quivira Golf Club is Jack Nicklaus' most recent design in Cabo San Lucas. The course and the accompanying Pueblo Bonito Resorts and Spas is located just north of Cabo San Lucas and immediately

south of the Dunes Course in Diamante. I saw two of the fairways from the southern most holes of the Dunes and it looks spectacular with the fairways high above the Pacific on low mountains and high dunes. Quivira claims to have more oceanfront exposure that any other course in Los Cabos, but having played the Dunes course at Diamante, I do not see how that is possible. I do feel however that the site offers dazzling views and breathtaking drops from tee to fairways and greens.

3. Cabo San Lucas Country Club, one of the oldest layouts in Los Cabos, was initially known as Raven Golf Club. This Roy Dye makeover is set amid palo blanca trees, endless cacti and bougainvillea. With views of the Sea of Cortez and El Arco, it offers a less expensive choice for a picturesque round of golf.

4. Puerto Los Cabos in San Jose del Cabo has two courses one by Jack Nicklaus and another by Greg Norman. Both courses are set along a three mile stretch on the Sea Of Cortez.

Well, I believe I've given one a good overview of the great golfing experiences in Los Cabos, Mexico and will move on to the only other course I've played in Mexico.

San Carlos Country Club Golf Course, Guaymas, Sonora, Mexico

One of my friends in Montgomery, Alabama who manufactured auto parts for Chrysler Motors, had a plant in Guaymas, Mexico. He offered his house to me and my good friend Alabama State Senator Larry Dixon and our families for spring break in 1990. Since his plant employed 450 people and was one of the biggest industries in this town, we were treated like royalty by the people and by his plant managers. Guaymas is located on the mainland of Mexico and about halfway down the eastern coast of the Sea of Cortez. When it was too rough to fish or sail, we played golf at this course. It was designed by Pete Dye in 1977 and has views of the Sea of Cortez and the landmark Teta Kasi Mountains. The latter are sharp twin peaks that resemble female breasts from the course.

This course is a flat, par 72 layout, with the outgoing nine rotating counterclockwise and returning to the clubhouse. The better incoming nine rotates clockwise. The absence of water hazards and the flat terrain make it fairly uninteresting, but we made up for that by drinking tequila at the nineteenth hole the two days we played here.

Ranking of the of the seven courses played in Mexico.

1. Querencia Golf Club, # 52
2. Cabo del Sol Golf Club, #62
3. Diamante Golf Club, #85
4. El Dorado Golf Club
5. Palmilla Golf Club
6. Cabo Real Golf Club
7. San Carlos Country and Golf Club

I hesitate to do a sample itinerary to Los Cabos, since I have described the situation with which a certain hotel is connected with a golf course, but it is a fluid and ever changing situation. Unless you know a Discovery Land owner, you have no access to El Dorado and Chileno Bay. Querencia and Diamante are ultra private and even if you know a member they must arrange for a member to host you. So that's still a problem playing these two wonderful courses. That leaves Cabo del Sol Ocean and Desert, the courses at Cabo Real, and possibly Palmilla to arrange. You can also stay at Quivira Resort and of course play that course. My advice is to investigate where you want to play and stay in a property that has an arrangement with those courses.

Chapter 7

New Zealand

This will be a short chapter since I've only played two courses on the North Island in New Zealand, the two courses owned by Julian Robertson. I believe, for the traveling golfer, it's worth the fifteen or so hour flight to play Cape Kidnappers and Kauri Cliffs. On our trip to Australia and New Zealand, Faye and I spent two weeks in Australia and only eight days in New Zealand. This was definitely not enough time to see, do and play the courses of New Zealand. If I could take my five grandchildren and Faye with me I would move there tomorrow. Everyone was friendly, had a smile on their faces, had a job and complained about nothing!

Located in the Southern Hemisphere, New Zealand's climate is just the opposite of the Northern Hemisphere's. The North Island, closer to the equator has a more temperate climate while the South Island gets colder temperatures the further south you go. The capital city, Wellington, is located in the North, but the major city in the North Island and hub for airline traffic is Auckland. The principal city in the South Island is Christchurch, but there are more resort cities in the South, the most popular of which is Queenstown. (Figure 57)

Cape Kidnappers is a high headland at the south-eastern end of Hawke's Bay on the east coast of the North Island. It's approximately twelve miles south of Napier and ten miles east of Hastings. The area's two major towns, known as the "Twin Cities" of New Zealand, have a combined population of 130,000.

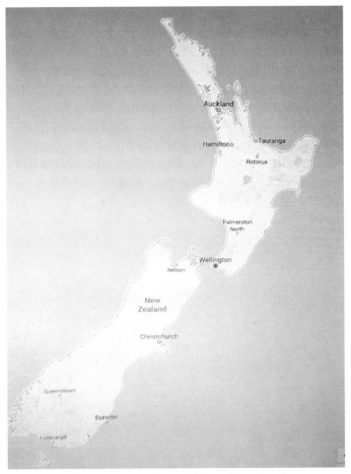

Figure 57. Map of New Zealand

Napier has a unique concentration of late 1930's art deco architecture as a result of the 1931 Hawke's Bay earthquake which destroyed much of the city. A number of very nice lodging options exist in Hastings for visitors who come, not only for the golf, but for bird watching, as the cape is a breeding site for over 3,000 pairs of Australasian gannets. Also vineyards and wineries here are popular tourist destinations.

The headland is named Cape Kidnappers because a servant of Captain Cook's HMS Endeavour crew was kidnapped October 15,1769, by a local Maori native tribe during a landfall there. The captured servant probably was to provide their evening meal until the crew opened fire on a Maori canoe, killing two tribesmen, at which time the servant jumped back into the water and swam back to the ship. Cook described the cape as having steep white cliffs with two large rocks resembling hay stacks near the headland. (Figure 58)

Figure 58. The headland at Cape Kidnappers as seen from the fifth green

Cape Kidnappers Golf Club, Hawke's Bay, New Zealand

Cape Kidnappers Golf Course, designed by Tom Doak in 2004, is truly a wonder to behold. It's Torrey Pines on steroids, lots and lots of steroids. The course is designed along a series of ridges jutting out toward the edge of the cliffs and rising 155 yards straight up from the waters of Hawke's Bay. The land gently slopes toward the ocean and the ridges are separated from one another by deep ravines. A stray shot will fall into these ravines if not stopped by strategically placed sand bunkers. The course is seaside golf at its finest, playing in windy conditions and on firm fast fairways. The course is not a true links as it is surrounded by dunes but playing on bluffs above the ocean. Quoting Tom Doak: "Our goal in designing golf courses is to create interesting holes you wouldn't find anywhere else." That wasn't hard to do at Cape Kidnappers because the site is not like anywhere else in golf. It's a much better golf course than Old Head, the elevation is similar, but the variety of scenery is much better.

The first hole is a demanding par four measuring 440 yards with the right side of the green dropping off dramatically into the deepest bunker you can imagine. If you are right you would rather be in the bunker than in a stand of pines to the right of it. I've been there and it was no fun. The second is a 550 yard par five with a relatively flat green with red farm sheds in the background. The routing after heading inland heads back toward Hawke's Bay with a "Wee Three" hole of 156 yards with a green severely sloping to the left. The fourth is an uphill par four with a blind tee shot followed by a green giving an intermediate view of the ocean. The fifth is a par four divided by two deep fairway bunkers sitting on a cliff above Hawke's Bay. (Figure 59)

Figure 59. The fifth green at Cape Kidnappers with Hawke's Bay in the near background and the eastern shore of the North Island in the far background

The first shot across the deep ravines is located at the par three sixth. This is one of four shots that requires the perilous leap from the end of one ridge to the adjacent one. The seventh is another long par four, turning back inland. The downhill second shot to a narrow green here is one of the most exciting on the course. The second leap of faith shot across the ravines comes at the par three eighth which requires a carry of 170 yards. I hit a driver, but the long hitters have no need to worry, as the name of the hole implies; "backstop" has a ridge that will stop most shots that go long. The 410 yard par four ninth returns to the clubhouse, and long hitters should consider hitting less than a driver to avoid the deep dip in the fairway.

The incoming nine begins in a way that reminds me of the tenth at Wade Hampton. Whenever I have a first time guest with me I always say: "You have not seen anything yet; wait until you see the incoming nine". The same statement can be made on the tenth tee here. This nine holes is beyond belief. It starts at the tenth, a 470 yard par four with Hawke's Bay as a backdrop, then moves to the eleventh, a 201 yard par three, which demands a long shot across yet another shallow ravine to the left of the tee. The course then begins to zig-zag back and forth with the longer holes headed toward the edge of the cliffs and the shorter ones headed back inland.

The twelfth, a par four 440 yard magnificent hole, is the most wide open fairway on the layout and positioned on a narrow ridge overlooking Hawke's Bay. The architecture is like a symphony with the tenth and eleventh like a gentle sonata. The shortest hole on the course, the par three thirteenth, has a dome shaped green that is hard to hit and requires another shot across a ravine just off the tee. The last leap of faith is the tee shot on the short par four fourteenth. The tee shot needs to be lined up way right, otherwise with any fade, you will be hitting three on the tee side of a deep gully. These two holes resemble bold symphonic movements. The crescendo of Cape Kidnappers' symphony occurs at the long 650 yard par five fifteenth. There is a 155 yard drop off to the left and another 22 yard drop off to the right side of the fairway, so the straight ball is in high demand here. The green sits on a promontory above the sea that the word 'dramatic' understates. (Figure 60)

Figure 60. The headland cliffs from the fifteenth green at Cape Kidnappers

The second par five on this nine, sixteen, boasts a tee sitting on yet another promontory further out on the cliff and its fairway is anticlimactic to the fifteenth hole. On the seventeenth fairway, a 460 yard par four, you have a beautiful view of the rolling hills covered with pale brown grasses and green pines. The eighteenth, a 480 yard par four, has a punchbowl green, offset to the right of the fairway. You want to be below the hole as balls above it might roll off the front edge of the green. You probably guessed that I loved this course and have it rated fifteenth (15) in my list of favorites. I will close this course narrative with a quote from Tom Doak. "Enjoy your game, and enjoy the setting. You will never play golf somewhere like this again." To this I only add, Amen.

Before we leave this venue I have one story to tell. I was so excited to get to Cape Kidnappers that I forgot my camera and left it at our hotel. Faye went back to get it while I played the outgoing nine with a caddie. She discovered that my battery was dead and charged it in the beautiful ladies locker room and lounge. While there she heard the familiar voice of Kathy Strong, wife of my friend Stan Strong of Houston, Texas and member of Wade Hampton. We had a nice visit in the lounge and met them the next day at a mountain overlook to admire the magnificent scenery that is the essence of New Zealand. Always remember that it's a small world! You never know when a friend might show up.

Kauri Cliffs Golf Course, Matauri Bay, Northland, New Zealand

Kauri Cliffs is located just below the northern tip of the North Island. It's some four hours north east of Auckland and approximately ten hours via auto from its sister course, Cape Kidnappers. The well-healed can take the resort's helicopter, but others would be well advised to fly to Keriken/Bay of Islands Airport near the Lodge at Kauri Cliffs. There is no lodging close to the resort, so staying in one of the Lodge's twenty-two guest suites is a must. The Lodge itself affords one a 180 degree view of the Pacific Ocean from a high cliff above the eighteenth and ninth greens. As I related earlier in the chapter, Cape Kidnappers is Torrey Pines on steroids and Kauri Cliffs is Pebble Beach and Turnberry on steroids. The views of the ocean and small islands from the cliffs are unlike anything else I've ever seen! (Figure 61)

Figure 61. View of several small islands looking north
west from the fifteenth fairway at
Kauri Cliffs

Kauri Cliffs was designed and built by David Harman's
firm who also designed and built dozens of courses in
the US and overseas. Sadly he died at an early age,
cutting his design career short. The par 72, 7,120
yard course was completed in 2001 and was
designated the Best New International Course in 2001
by "Golf Digest". It currently stands at number thirty-
nine in "Golf Digest Top 100 Greatest Golf Courses in
the World".

Fifteen holes in the layout have views of the Pacific
Ocean and Matauri Bay. The outgoing nine rotates in
a counterclockwise fashion, with the seventh and
eighth on a cliff just above a secluded beach, "Pink
Beach", and its churning waves. (Figure 62)

Figure 62. Looking south from the seventh tee at
Kauri Cliff's "Pink Beach"

The opening hole's tee is located in front of the Lodge
and presents a straight away, uphill, par four that
heads into rolling farmland. The second and third
holes are back and forth par fours whose fairways are
parallel, with the latter the requisite short par four.
The fourth is a long par five dogleg right that gives
one a beautiful, long range view of the bay. A recent
renovation by Rees Jones changed the fifth hole from
a long par three with a forced carry into a shorter par
three that requires a 'drop shot" from an elevated tee.
The sixth is another dogleg par four whose green
overlooks the demanding par three seventh that hugs
and hangs over the cliff. The par five eighth is a
magnificent hole along the cliff's edge with the bay on
the right. The outgoing nine's ninth is a severely uphill par four with a gully, similar to Cape Kidnappers'
trademark ravines, just off the tee. It's easily carried

with a decent tee shot, but intimidates us duffers. The ninth ends up essentially back at the Lodge but below the eighteenth green.

The incoming nine rotates clockwise and starts off toward the north into marsh land and forest. The tenth is a relatively short par four and the eleventh, a longer par four, is bordered by wetlands, palm and totara trees. The thirteenth is an uphill par four that climbs to the apex of the property. From the elevated tee at fourteen begins the most dramatic stretch of five holes all perched on a high ledge overlooking Matauri Bay. The par three fourteenth looks down on the Cavalli Islands, (See Figure 61.) while the par five fifteenth and the par four sixteenth both dogleg left around the bay, sweeping downhill in dramatic fashion. (Figure 63.) The seventeenth is another dogleg left par four that again hugs the cliffs above the Bay. The eighteenth is another uphill battle par five that ends at the base of the Lodge. Looking down on these two finishing holes I wonder if there is a better view anywhere in golf.

In 2008 and 2009 Cape Kidnappers and Kauri Cliffs both hosted the Kiwi Challenge. These matches featured golfers, all under thirty years of age, from this part of the world. Among them were Hunter Mahan, Brandt Snedeker, Anthony Kim, Adam Scott and Sean O'Hair. In 2008 Mahan defeated Kim in a playoff, and in 2009 Kim defeated O'Hair, again in a playoff. Kauri Cliffs also hosted the "Shell's Wonderful World of Golf" match in 2003. I have this course listed

Figure 63. The sweeping downhill par four sixteenth at
Kauri Cliffs with Matauri Bay and the
south east coast in the background

eighteenth in my list of favorites, one above Pebble
Beach Golf Links. I sincerely believe it's that good!

Before I leave Kauri Cliffs I, as usual, have a story to
tell. The second round, I played with Michael Harger,
a member of the Clemson University Golf Team, who
was interning here for his winter semester. He related
that several weeks earlier an American billionaire,
who shall go nameless, was over in his Gulfstream
with friends and his brother-in-law. They all came out
to play here. All bought shoes, tees etc. but didn't buy
any balls. The staff wondered about this until another
employee saw the brother-in-law scooping up range
balls for them to play with. I suppose that is why he
has billions of dollars, as golf balls over here are
expensive, $24 per sleeve for Pro V1's.

Other courses on The North Island, New Zealand

1. Titirangi Golf Club. Located twenty-five minutes from Auckland City Center and on the western coast of New Zealand, the course is situated between the Waitakere Mountain Range and Maunkau Harbor. The Club was organized in 1909 and in 1927 Alister MacKenzie was commissioned to redesign the course, his only work in New Zealand.
2. Gulf Harbour Country Club. Located on the Hauraki Gulf just north west of Auckland, this property is relatively close to Titirangi Golf Club and could make for a good two day destination while staying in Auckland. The course was designed by Robert Trent Jones Jr. in 1997 and has great views of the Hauraki Gulf.
3. The Kinloch Club. Located in the exact center of the main body of the North Island some three hours south of Auckland, it is situated on the largest fresh water lake in New Zealand, Lake Taupo. This is a major resort with a first class Jack Nicklaus signature golf course.
4. Wairakei Golf Club. Located very close to the Kinloch Club in the center of the North Island, this course is situated in an environmental sanctuary. The course was designed in 1970 by Peter Thomson in the Lake Taupo area and the two courses would make a good location for a golf outing on the North Island.
5. Paraparaumu Beach Golf Club. Located due north of Wellington, this course, designed by Alex Russell in 1949, is a good links course in sandy soil similar to the links courses in the UK and Ireland. Russell collaborated with Alister MacKenzie in design-

ing Royal Melbourne. The views with a low mountain range in the background, are said to be spectacular.
6. Tara Iti Golf Club, Mangawhai, New Zealand. Built on a sandy spit of land ninety (90) minutes north of Auckland, this is the latest concoction of Renaissance Golf Design and Tom Doak. The site was cleared of dense pines and brought back to the natural sand dunes and native vegetation. It opened in October 2015 and if the pictures do it justice, it's comparable to Pine Valley. This is yet another reason to visit New Zealand for golf on the North Island and fun on the South Island.

Other courses on the South Island, New Zealand:

Three of the top courses on the South Island are located essentially in Queenstown. Of all the places that Faye and I have visited, this is without a doubt in the top ten for variety and total coolness. From ski resorts to golf courses, from Milford Sound (The Southern Alps' answer to Norwegian Fjords) to Skippers Canyon, the latter houses the Shotover River, the origin of the New Zealand gold rush and site of the first bungy jump. If you go to New Zealand do not miss these two sites!!

1. Clearwater Golf Club. Just outside of Christchurch this course, designed around a number of fresh water lakes, opened in 2002. Designed by Sir Bob Charles, it's home of the New Zealand Womens Open.
2. Millbrook Resort. This is now a 27 hole golf complex designed by Sir Bob Charles and renovated in 2010 by Greg Turner. The course offers unbeliev-

able scenery at the base of The Remarkables Mountain Range just outside of Queenstown.

3. The Hills Golf Club. Designed by Darby Partners in 2007 and twenty minutes from Queenstown, this is what I would call a big golf course which spans a glacial valley with dramatic elevation changes.

4. Jack's Point Golf Club. The newest course in Queenstown is probably the most dramatic. Bounded by the Remarkables Mountain Range and Lake Wekatipu, it weaves through grasslands and dramatic rock outcroppings.

As far as the ranking of the two courses I played in New Zealand, I have thought long and hard regarding this. Initially I had Kauri Cliffs rated higher, but finally decided that Cape Kidnappers is better and have it listed fifteenth in my list of favorites. Kauri Cliffs checks in at eighteenth in this list.

As I have done in several chapters, I will give the reader a sample itinerary. With new additions of courses on the North Island, it may be worthwhile to spend the better part of a week playing the headliner courses on the North Island. If one decided to do that, say on a buddies trip, I would definitely take a second week in New Zealand exploring Queenstown and the South Island.

A Sample Itinerary for Golf in New Zealand

Flying from the west coast of America, one arrives in Auckland in the early morning. You are still four hours from Melbourne and over three hours from Sydney. Assuming you've had a good night's sleep, I would rent a car and drive to Titirangi.

Day 1. Play Titirangi Golf Club; it's twenty minutes north of the airport and a good starting point.
Overnight here or travel one hour on up to Tara Iti.
Day 2. Play Tara Iti GC, the newest and rated the best course in New Zealand.
Day 3. Drive to Kauri Cliffs and play it that day. It's a four hour drive, maybe less.
Day 4. Play Kauri Cliffs again and fly to Napier-Hastings Airport in Hastings.
Day 5. Play Cape Kidnappers.
Day 6. I would repeat the round at Kidnappers; after all that's why you came here.
Day 7. You could either backtrack and play the two courses adjacent to Lake Taupo, Kinloch and Wairakei, or fly on to Queenstown. You should definitely spend the better part of a second week here on the South Island.

Chapter VIII

Australia

In February 2008 Faye and I traveled to Australia on Air New Zealand from Los Angeles and after thirteen hours arrived in Auckland. The distances are mind boggling because you are still four hours from Melbourne. We only visited the south-east corner of Australia and still the distances between cities there alone is unbelievable. For example, flights from Melbourne to Tasmania take one hour, from Melbourne to Adelaide, although it looks short on the map, take slightly over one hour. Our flight from Adelaide to Sydney took two hours. Looking at the map (Figure 64) you would not have expected the distances to be so great.

Traveling to Australia, you cross the International Date Line so you lose one day going over. In other words we left Los Angeles at 9:00pm on February 21, 2008 and arrived in Melbourne at 9:30am on February 23, 2008 We were refreshed, having slept in the bunk type beds in business class, and ready to explore the southern Australian coast. I suppose you could do coach with all the potential upgrades, but I would not recommend it. You cannot plan well without a golf travel agency, and I highly recommend Gary Lisborn at Golf Select. He met our plane in Melbourne, showed us to our rental car and had all destinations, including all golf courses, programmed into the GPS.

We checked into The Langham Hotel located in central Melbourne. This location was perfect for sightseeing and for quick access to The Sandbelt

Area for golf as well as close to the Royal Victorian
Eye and Ear Hospital where I spent the first two days
participating in my Continuing Medical Education.
Faye had a more exciting time. While having

Figure 64. Map of Australia and Tasmania

breakfast in the Langham's club room, she was
seated across from the singer Rod Stewart and his
wife Penny. That was the highlight of her trip.

Having researched the one best thing to do, we
started the day driving out The Great Ocean Road

which runs for 600 miles from Melbourne to Adelaide, two of Australia's three major cities. This road makes the 76 miles of California's Big Sur look almost insignificant and runs westward along the shore of The Indian Ocean. The brutal surf and winds pound the malleable lime and sandstone shore, eating away at the Australian coastline and leaving mile after mile of sweeping vistas of sculpted cliffs, towers and arches framed against the turquoise sea. (Figure 65)

Figure 65. The Indian Ocean pounding the coastline and cliffs just west of Melbourne

Part I
Tasmania

To keep things organized, although we didn't travel to Tasmania first, I felt like I should discuss it first. You fly either to Launceston in the north or to Hobart in the south. Since we didn't have time for wildlife tours in Tasmania, we opted to fly to and stay in Launceston. I had spent all day in The Royal Victorian Eye and Ear Hospital observing several surgeries. Maybe I was tired from standing up all day, but I got into a major disagreement checking in with Jetstar our carrier from Melbourne to Tasmania, because of weight limitations on our bags. Local carriers in Australia have different rules depending on whether they are affiliated with Air New Zealand or Qantas, the two major carriers 'down under'. It was a hectic time moving clothes from our bags to my golf bag etc. Ask ahead is my advice.

This brings up another piece of golf travel advice. I put all of my folded golf shirts in gallon sized zip-lock bags, start sealing them, then sit on the bag; and finish sealing them. This maneuver flattens the shirt which then takes up much less room and dramatically helps with wrinkling. Another piece of travel advice, as above, is to check the weight restrictions on all flights; then you know when you need to quickly rearrange and move those sealed shirts in the zip-lock bags.

The city itself, named for Launceston in Cornwall England, is one of the oldest cities in Australia and has many historic buildings. The main attraction is Cataract Gorge, formed by the Tamar River, which we visited on our way back to the airport on our second full day here. It turned me off of chairlifts forever.

Barnbougle Dunes Golf Links, Bridport, Tasmania, Australia

Some forty miles north of Launceston, set amongst the wild and dramatic landscape directly on Tasmania's northeastern coast, lie the rolling fairways that became Barnbougle Dunes. The course is the brainchild of a small group of dreaming golfers led by Mike Clayton, an Australian and ex-European tour player. In 2004, he attracted the then up and coming golf architect, Tom Doak who helped him design the rolling coastal dunes that once had been a potato farm. Mr. Doak's minimalistic style was a perfect fit to complement the layout and enhance the beautiful natural landscape rather than distract from it. The fairways and greens are bent grass and the rough is primarily fescue. Both these grasses flourish in the coastal environment. Doak and Clayton have copied the style of the great links courses of Scotland and Ireland that I have discussed in the early chapters. Although the fairways are more generous than those of the courses in Great Britain and Ireland, the greens are similar to them with rolling, natural undulations that follow the coastal dunes closely.

The opening stretch of holes are some of the best opening holes in the world and remind me of the opening holes at County Down. The first is a long, fairly open par five. Two is a medium length par four; it is followed by another good 360 yard par four.

The fourth, a short par four of 280 yards, may be one of the best short par fours in the world. It plays into a prevailing headwind and has the largest bunker in the southern hemisphere to the right of the fairway.

Hitting short of the bunker is no picnic either as one is faced with a blind, steep uphill shot. The outward nine rotates clockwise and the last five holes, five through nine, are directly on the high dune ridge overlooking the beach. The walk from the fourth green to the fifth tee is one of the finest in golf along the path parallel to the Bass Strait. (Figure 66)

Figure 66. The path leading from the fourth green to the fifth tee; "on the beach" at Barnbougle Dunes

One of the real advantages of "The Dunes" is that higher handicapped golfers are encouraged to play a shorter course making it much more fun, at least it was for me. The next par three seventh is named "Tom's Little Devil". It's a wicked 125 yard par three that demands a precise shot from an elevated tee to a small upturned green. Miss it left and you are in a deep bunker; miss it long and you are down a steep bank. Come to think about it, this hole is exactly the same as the seventh at Royal County Down. The eighth is the longest par four on the course and the number one handicap hole. The inward nine is more open and may be more striking, with multiple panoramas of the course beginning at the tenth hole where the course turns slightly inland. (Figure 67)

Figure 67. Panorama of the start of the inward nine at Barnbougle Dunes

At the par four fifteenth, which parallels the manmade cut to the Bass Strait, the routing heads back to the ocean. The par three sixteenth is directly on the beach, with the dramatic seventeenth and eighteenth separated from the ocean with low grasses on a tidal plain to the right of the fairways. One of the great features of the course is the variability in playing conditions, depending on the time of day you play, as the inward nine rotates counterclockwise, just opposite to the incoming nine. I played in the morning when the wind was quiet and had a good score. In contrast, in the afternoon the wind tends to pick up and provides challenges on many of the closing holes, which again parallel the ocean. now on the right.

The rankings of Barnbougle Dunes were high from the start in 2005. It remains the number one course in Australia that has public access. It is rated fourth in Australia by "Australian Golf Digest" and number thirty-fourth in the world by U.S. "Golf Magazine". "Golf Digest" most recently rated it number eleven in the world, excluding American courses. I felt it was worth the trip over to Tasmania to play this course and now with its sister course, Lost Farm, adjacent to Barnbougle Dunes, I feel it's a must play venue if you travel to Australia for golf. I have it highly rated in my list of favorites at twenty-fifth.

Barnbougle Lost Farm, Bridpost, Tasmania, Australia

The sister course was conceived by the same group that initiated "The Dunes" except the design firm of Coore & Crenshaw was enlisted to design and build this course. Although located just across the river from its sister course, the land is actually a lost potato farm. The site is more dramatic, with steeper sand dunes than "The Dunes" but the minimalistic style of using the natural topography of the land to dictate the routing is similar. Lost Farm plays along the coast and inland and actually is composed of twenty holes. The first extra hole, 13a, was built as a substitute hole but once the course was completed everyone felt it was too good of a hole to leave it out of the routing. The other extra hole, 18a, serves as a bet equalizer; it is a very short hole that leads to the bar; maybe the name of the bar should be 'The 21st Hole.'

Part II
Melbourne

The sandbelt region of Melbourne, similar to the sandbelt area of North Carolina, are both perfect areas for growing grass and have great drainage; therefore they are also excellent areas for golf courses. Located just south east of the Melbourne City Center and lying on the eastern shore of Port Phillips Bay, is the Melbourne Sandbelt area. Some twenty million years ago the low lying areas were flooded here depositing sandstone material extending some 90 yards below the surface. This area in Melbourne, some 25 square miles of undulating land, is a mecca for world renowned golf courses. This region provides the rare opportunity to construct bent grass green complexes along with heavy lipped bunkers directly adjacent to the greens. The base grass of couch, noted for its firmness and lack of seasonal changes, provides the perfect environment for fairways.

The courses here, commonly referred to as the seven sisters, are all dramatic. Gary Lisborn had set up tee times for me on five of them: Royal Melbourne West and East, Kingston Heath, Metropolitan and Victoria, all in the top ten in Australia. The other three in this exclusive list are Yarra Yarra, Commonwealth and Huntingdale.

The Victoria Golf Club, Cheltenham, Victoria, Australia

This Club was founded and co-designed by William (Billy) Meader in 1903. Two years earlier he helped organize the Victoria Golf Association. The original course was located at Fisherman's Bend in Port Melbourne and co-designed by Oscar Damon, the first Club Captain. In 1926 the Club was moved to its current location and Alister MacKenzie was commissioned to refine the course and complete all of the dramatic bunkering lining the course and surrounding the greens, giving it the aesthetically distinctive character that is so stunning here at Royal Melbourne and at Kingston Heath. All three are very close together, with Victoria just across the street from Royal Melbourne. Mike Clayton has fairly recently restored the bunkering that is MacKenzie's legacy. (Figure 68)

The Victoria Club has had its share of famous golfers. First and foremost is the great Peter W. Thomson who won five Open Championships, three straight in a span of seven years, along with three Australian Opens and two World Cups. Doug Bachli is the club's most famous amateur golfer as the first Australian to win the British Amateur Championship

Figure 68. The fourth hole at Victoria illustrating
the bearded bunkers cut up to the green

while amassing two Australian Open Championships
and three Victorian Open Championships. Most
recently Geoff Ogilvy has carried the standard for The
Victorian Club, first as junior Champion of the Club,
then as the 1997 Victorian Amateur Champion and
finally the 2006 US Open Champion. He performed
the latter in dramatic fashion, defeating Phil
Mickelson, Jim Furyk and Colin Montgomerie by one
stroke at Winged Foot Golf Club.

The course layout is somewhat unusual in that the
first hole is a very short par four of 256 yards.
Driveable by most golfers, I was ecstatic to make a
par on the first hole I played in the Southern
Hemisphere. I played with a chap who was
competing in a blind match and I attested his score at

the eighteenth green. The next two holes are long par fours lined with thick tea trees and complex undulating greens. The fourth is a 180 yard uphill par three and the seventh is essentially similar with a blind tee shot. The closing two holes on the outward nine are composed of a shortish par five eighth that I managed to double bogey and another longer par five that for me is a four shotter. I did manage a bogey and turned to the incoming nine with no particular expectations.

Looking back at my photographs of this nine holes, it may be the most impressive nine in the sandbelt. I really had not had a chance to study these courses before this trip, as I was still working full time at breakneck speed. I didn't appreciate this classic layout with the bunkering and greens. The tenth swoops from right to left and uphill to a turtle back green. The eleventh is yet another uphill par four which shares bunkers with the short par four fifteenth. The twelfth moves from left to right downhill, and the thirteenth is a 430 yard par four with the number one handicapped ranking. These dramatic changes in topography are secondary to the course's design following the ancient dunes. The fourteenth is a 155 yard par three that demands an accurate shot to the turned up green complex; miss the green and bogey is a good score here.   The sixteenth is the longest par three, at 195 yards, that frequently requires a three wood to carry the green. Both nines end in par fives, the seventeenth being a very long par four. The eighteenth, at 510 yards, gives one a legitimate chance to make a birdie on the last hole.

Three Australian Mens and Womens Opens have been played here: the Mens in 1961, 1981 and most recently in 2002, the Womens having been staged here in 1974, 1976 and 2014. I have it ranked eighty-fourth in my list of favorites.

The Royal Melbourne Golf Club (West Course),
Black Rock, Victoria, Australia

Some fifteen years ago, while reading an article about Royal Melbourne and golf travel, mention was made that one could not consider himself a complete traveling golfer without making the pilgrimage to Royal Melbourne. Right then and there I made up my mind to play the two courses that make up Royal Melbourne. The West Course is always listed first in Australia's list of best courses and has been consistently in the top twenty of the world's best courses, having once been rated as high as fifth.

The Melbourne Golf Club was organized by five Scots in 1891: John Bruce, Tom Finlay and Hugh Playfair from St. Andrews along with William Knox and Tom Brentnall from Musselburgh. A desirable site was identified near the Caulfield Railway Station in the fringe of the sandbelt area and within six or seven weeks play began on Tom Finlay's layout here. A year later ladies were admitted as Associate Members. Within five years this site was landlocked with encroaching houses and another site eight miles further south was identified on a hill at Black Rock.

The second course's location, identified as the Sandringham property, was divided into land plots referred to as paddocks. So by 1925 the front three paddocks were sold and an adjoining large paddock was acquired in preparation of Alister MacKenzie's visit and subsequent design. This new land acquisition accommodated four holes on the West course and twelve holes on the later developed East Course.

So, in October of 1926 the good Doctor MacKenzie arrived in Melbourne, some six years before designing Cypress Point and Augusta National, to design Royal Melbourne's West course. The name Royal was acquired when HRH Queen Victoria granted this designation in 1895. MacKenzie was paid the sum equivalent to $2,000 for his work at Royal Melbourne, but while here consulted on a number of other courses in the sandbelt area, as we will discuss. Alex Russell a local member and Mick Morcom, the Greenskeeper from 1905 to 1935, assisted with this design and construction.

In his 1920 book "Golf Architecture", MacKenzie outlined 13 principle features of an ideal golf course. In various ways he incorporated all of these into his design here. Blake Griffith always said: "I'm not going to hunt for any of your balls Kitchens". So, to me MacKenzie's most important principle is: "there should be a complete absence of the annoyance and irritation caused by the necessity of searching for golf balls". He was interested in what he called "strategic design" i.e., that a player had to use his brain with strategic routes and/or alternate routes depending on his skill and length and decide whether to take a bold or timid approach to each hole. He also liked dogleg holes. As testimony to that end, the third, fourth, sixth, tenth, eleventh, twelve, seventeenth and eighteenth are all doglegs. Five are left and three are right. The primary reason that so many of his courses are rated so highly is that he emphasized that his courses should have beautiful natural surroundings with even the hazards having a natural appearance.

His basic layout has remained the same since opening in 1931. Only the seventh has been totally redesigned by Ivo Whitton in 1937 and Whitton also moved the first and twelfth greens along with any number of bunkers. The first is a par four running downhill from the clubhouse. The second is a great risk and reward par five. The single digit golfer can bite off as much as he likes on this slightly dogleg right to carry the large bunker on the right at the corner of the dogleg. The fourth is another par five, designed around a large sand dune; it is a magnificent uphill, often photographed hole. Indeed, all of the par fives are reachable in two but demand precise shotmaking and strategic planning. The fifth is without a doubt the most famous par three in the Southern Hemisphere. The undulating green, sloping from back to front and set in its own natural amphi-theater, is framed by natural bush and deep bunkers that encroach the green circumferentially. One must be below the hole here and everywhere on this course. (Figure 69)

The sixth is a markedly dogleg right par four with a magnificent stretch of heathland and sand waste inside the turn off the tee. The seventh is a 165 yard uphill par three with a huge bunker just off the right side of the green. As with most of MacKenzie's greens here, the slope is from back to front forcing one to risk the hazards to avoid being above the holes. The ninth is designed up and over another large sand dune to a green protected by two

Figure 69. The dramatic fifth hole on Royal
Melbourne's West Course

large bunkers to the left and two smaller bunkers to
the right and long.

The tenth begins a stretch of three dogleg holes, the
first of which is a driveable par four of only 310 yards.
The caveat here: one must avoid the ever present
bunker, in the dogleg as well as in a waste area
known as Australia's "Hell's Half Acre". The twelfth is
a par five for the members but in tournaments here,
plays as a par four. It has a huge nest of bunkers in
the dogleg on the left.

The West Course then crosses a road to a second
paddock and continues the routing with a short par
three thirteenth. It demands a precise shot, as the
middle of the green is raised, and any misdirected ball

will end up in a bunker. The other three holes on this adjoining paddock are the par four fourteenth, which has nine bunkers surrounding the green, the par five fifteenth, which has cross mounds and bunkers 100 yards short of a raised green, and the long par three sixteenth which has the flattest green surface here. Moving back across the road to the primary paddock is the seventeenth, another par four that has two bunkers guarding the line to the hole, one at 150 yards off the tee and another 100 yards past the first. The less accomplished player, myself included, is satisfied to have the tee shot shunted to the right and then plays short and left of the green hoping to chip up and make a par. The eighteenth is yet another blind shot par four with the line off the tee marked by a big oval bunker imbedded into the dune. Cross bunkers, cut well back from the front of the green, demand a perfect approach second or, in my case, third shot to a left to right sloping green.

The Royal Melbourne Composite Course

In 1959 when Royal Melbourne was chosen to host The World Cup matches, known at the time as the Canada Cup, the leaders at Royal Melbourne decided that it would be best to have the routing stay in the primary paddock of the club. To accomplish that goal, twelve holes were selected from the West Course and six holes selected from the East Course. This was easily accomplished as the courses were intertwined at two locations in the big paddock. Alex Russell, an Australian pro and member here, and Mike Morcom, the superintendent here, designed the East course some five years after helping MacKenzie with the West Course.

So the Composite Course starts out with numbers one and two of the West Course, the latter having a par of four rather than five. Since both courses start at the clubhouse and the second green is very close to the first tee on the East, the third hole on the Composite is the short par four first from the East. It's a 330 yard hole from an elevated tee with a large bunker to the right of the landing area. The fourth incorporates the second hole from the East, a dogleg to the right with a difficult uphill shot to the large, very fast green. Both of the wonderful par threes on the front side of the West are the same, along with the sixth.

I'm not going to explain all of the changes but the par four third of the East, a downhill potential birdie, is the fifteenth. The wonderful par three fourth on the East is the sixteenth here. It's a long par three, the only one on the incoming nine. As usual, it is well bunker-ed on the front but long; it can easily lead to a three putt. I hit the best shot of the trip on this hole for a rare birdie.

The round finishes with the long par five from seventeenth on the East, which is another risk reward par five. The last hole in play, the eighteenth on the East parallels the first on the West and is adjacent to the clubhouse; it is the eighteenth on the Composite Course. It has been described as the best finishing hole in Australia.

Not surprisingly, Royal Melbourne has hosted sixteen Australian Opens, two World Cup of Golf events, in 1959 and 1972, and two Presidents Cups. In 1998, in the first Presidents Cup held outside the United States, the Cup was won by the international team captained by Peter Thomson. The second Presidents Cup hosted here in 2011 was won by by the United States. I have the West Course along with the six holes from the East Course that make up the composite course ranked tenth in my list of favorites.

The Royal Melbourne (East Course), Black Rock, Victoria, Australia

As mentioned, in 1931, Alex Russell, a well known pro golfer who won The Australian Open in 1924 and the Victorian Open in 1925, along with Mick Morcom, the longstanding superintendent, designed the East Course. The East Course starts and finishes in the main paddock with six of the seven holes in this location included in The Composite Course. These holes have been described above and include some of the most dramatic undulations found on either of the courses. After the fourth, the routing moves to the second paddock and after two holes it moves to the third paddock. After moving through these two paddocks this course becomes somewhat flatter and more mundane.

The par threes on the East are closer to MacKenzie's design and its routing includes four short par fours, four mid length par fours and four long par fours. The playing style on the East is entirely different from that of the West. The bunkers are not as deep and not as difficult to hit from and the fairways are not as wide. I would recommend playing it simply to experience the six holes that are included in the Composite Course, as they are some of the best holes in this routing. I have not listed the East Course in my list of favorites.

Kingston Heath Golf Club, Cheltenham, Victoria, Australia

Another MacKenzie gem, Kingston Heath is consistently rated as number two in Australia. This course was originally designed by Dan Soutar in 1925. When Dr. MacKenzie visited here in 1926, he refined the course and provided a suitable bunkering strategy that is the hallmark of this magnificent course. Soutar designed the original layout so one wouldn't be required to play into the afternoon sun, and Mick Morcom, the superintendent at Royal Melbourne, actually oversaw the building of the course.

The first hole, a difficult 450 yard par four, begins with an uphill tee shot over bunkers on the right side of the landing area. After another par four, the third is a distinctive short par four of less than 300 yards. This represents a driveable par four hole, but because the green is shallow and angled to hold only the most precise shot, the penalties for missing the green are severe. The only par three on the outgoing nine, the fifth, shows an original green with the bumps and hollows preserved and is protected by six surrounding bunkers. Fairway bunkers at Kingston Heath are beautiful yet penal, since the sand is shallow and the lips are high and bearded with grass. (Figure 70)

There are three par threes on the incoming nine, the tenth, the fifteenth and/or the nineteenth, which is also a short alternate hole. The fifteenth is probably the signature hole at Kingston Heath. Originally it was a short par four with a blind tee shot over a hill. MacKenzie didn't like the hole and redesigned it, bringing the green forward to the top of the dune

Figure 70. An example of the classic bunkering on number one that is the hallmark of Kingston Heath

and making it a demanding short par three. He surrounded the green with severe bunkers which require real competence when extracting oneself from them. (Figure 71) In the 1995 Australian Open, Greg Norman clinched the victory with a perfect, low, five iron shot here to within ten feet. The fourteenth has been described as one of the best par fives in Australia, measuring 566 yards. Here I hit three career shots and made a long putt for my second birdie of the trip. The incoming nine finishes with the long 467 yard par four, seventeenth distinctive in that it has no bunkers, and finally with the 430 yard par four eighteenth.

Figure 71. Kingston Heath's fifteenth, probably
the signature hole here

Kingston Heath has hosted nine Australian Opens,
two Australian Masters and most recently the 2016
World Cup of Golf. I have it listed forty-seventh in my
list of favorites.

The Metropolitan Golf Club, South Oakleigh, Victoria,
Australia

Metropolitan dates its origin back to 1891 when the
original members formed The Royal Melbourne Golf
Club near the Cauldfield railway station. In 1896,
when Royal Melbourne moved into the sandbelt area
of Black Rock, some of the members stayed at the
original location and formed The Cauldwell Golf Club.
In 1906 this club bought a farm in Oakleigh and in
1908 the members moved to the new site and changed the name to The Metropolitan Golf Club. Designed
by engineer-member, J. B. MacKenzie (no relation to

Alister MacKenzie), the farmland was transformed into one of the best golf courses in Australia.

The course has the reputation as one of the most beautiful and best conditioned courses in Australia; many refer to it as the Augusta of Australia. The fairways are immaculate couch grass, a spongy soft grass that makes a perfect surface. The large, fast bent grass greens come right up to the greenside bunkers. This unusual feature makes the green complexes very dramatic and unforgiving.

Almost every hole is flanked by stands of native Australian trees and shrubs which harbor many species of native birds. The course is famous for a specimen of a red flowering gum tree which in February buds out with flaming red blooms. This tree is part of the Club's logo. In 1926 Dr. Alister Mac-Kenzie visited here and made suggestions to improve the routing. The course has undergone two other renovations, one by Dick Wilson in 1960 and another by Michael Clayton in 2006. Sadly much of Alister MacKenzie's work and essentially all of Wilson's work was wiped out when this land was taken from the Club for a school development.

Most of us have played golf until the dark of evening at a special course or during a match, but to play this course and get to my planned meeting at The Royal Victoria Eye and Ear Hospital at 1:00 pm, I actually teed off at dawn. It was a wonderful experience with only myself and a pleasant caddie; we really had the course to ourselves. The first hole is a par four that sweeps downhill from the club house. I managed to hit the green but three putted for a bogey. The second, a 175 yard par three, is another great hole as is the unusual par four fifth. The outgoing nine holes contain the best undulating ground and are much better than the incoming nine much of which was lost in the school development. The remaining land for the new incoming nine's site is flat and contains parallel holes with only the last two par four holes resembling the better outgoing nine.

American golfer Gene Sarazen won the 1936 Australian Open here and the great Peter Thomson began his career with a win here in the 1951 Australian Open. Other tournaments of note are the 1968 Australian PGA when Ken Nagle narrowly defeated the Big Three, Palmer, Nicklaus and Player. American Brad Faxon won the 1993 Australian Open here and lastly, in 1997 Lee Westwood beat Greg Norman in a playoff in the same tournament. I do not have Metropolitan listed in my list of favorites.

Other courses in the Melbourne Area:
I've mentioned the names of the other well known courses in the sandbelt area, however, some 60 miles from Melbourne City Center is The National Golf Club. It is located at Cape Schanck on Victoria's Mornington Peninsula due south of the sandbelt area. Started in 1985 as a country club, Robert Trent Jones, Jr. first designed The Old Course here which opened in 1988. It's reported to be a dramatic course with unsurpassed views of the coastline of Port Phillips Bay. The other courses located at this club are the Norman designed Moonah, an inland tract with great views of the rolling land, and The Ocean Course designed by Thomson, Wolveridge and Perrett. This course I would like to see, since I like links courses so much and it has a natural links beginning in the lowlands

and ascending up the high dunes and back down again.

If I go back to Melbourne I would want to see The National Golf Club, but considering the quality of those I've already discussed in Australia and New Zealand, I wouldn't recommend it on anyone's initial visit "down under".

Part III
Adelaide and Sydney

I came to Adelaide to visit and observe a very famous endoscopic sinus surgeon who operates all over the world and is a magician with the endoscopic operating techniques. Being in the surgical suite with him was like watching an artist paint a beautiful picture. My only regret is that I didn't see him operate until the end of my surgical career, as I could have adopted some of his methods. I was very busy observing him, playing golf and visiting the many wineries in the area, as much of the Australian wines exported to the United States are produced here. Visiting Adelaide gave Faye and me the whole package of South Australia and the wine region, but now, back to golf.

The Royal Adelaide Golf Club, Seaton,
South Australia, Australia

The original Club was founded in 1870 by two Members of Parliament with the Governor of Australia, Sir James Fergusson, as its patron. When Sir James was recalled to the UK in 1873, the Club declined and folded in 1876. Another Club was started in 1892 on the North Parklands in Glenelg, but moved to the sandy craters and dunes of Seaton in 1904 where it remains today. The title of Royal was granted in 1923. The clubhouse is literally just behind and adjacent to the western railway line. Dr. Alister MacKenzie added his finishing touches to the layout during his visit "down under" in 1926. The location in Seaton, some twenty minutes from the city center and slightly over one mile from the coast, prompted him to state: "No seaside courses I have seen possess such magnificent sand craters as those at Royal Adelaide."

Royal Adelaide is a very open links course rarely found in Australia or for that matter, the UK. I wouldn't let the openness fool you as it poses more problems than one would think of on first appearance. It's a combination of testing short holes; numbers one, three and ten are all short par fours. There are only three par threes with the seventh, a wonderful par three hole, the only one on the outgoing nine. The two par threes on the incoming nine are the twelfth and sixteenth; both are long holes, the former 222 yards and the latter 181 yards. Even in 2008, the sixteenth required a driver for my tee shot. The four par fives, numbers two and nine, on the outgoing nine and the fifteenth and seventeenth on the incoming nine, are all over 500 yards long and the course measures out at as a 7,258 yard par 73.

Two holes demand further discussion. First, the short par four third is a MacKenzie gem and is an introduction to the sand dunes that follow. The natural dunes give the third all the requirements necessary for a great two shotter. From an elevated tee and adjacent to the railway line, one must decide whether to attempt to drive the hole, an impossibility for me, or to play short. The tee shot is blind and a poorly struck shot will fall short of the natural mound leaving one a blind approach to a narrow, angled green, guarded at the left by a steep embankment. It's MacKenzie's gift and legacy to Royal Adelaide. The other standout hole on the outgoing nine is the 183 yard par three seventh. There is a large, vicious waste area off the tee and a ring of five bunkers in front of the elevated green, along with two bunkers both left and right at the back one-third of the green. This green has an ample landing area, sloping from back to front, but a shot over the green will likely end up lost. (Figure 72) I have not included Royal Adelaide in my list of favorites.

Figure 72. The seventh green at Royal Adelaide with a large waste area followed by a ring of bunkers guarding the elevated green

Kooyonga Golf Club, May Terrace, Lockleys, SA, Australia

It was in the early planning stages of this Australian trip that Gary Lisborn mentioned a course unknown to me - Kooyonga. He told me that this course was a wonderful example of a championship golf course in the rich sandy soil just fifteen minutes from Adelaide's City Center. Indeed this Club, Royal Adelaide, The Grange and Glenelg Golf Clubs are all within a ten mile radius of each other in a sand belt area similar to the one found in Melbourne.

Kooyonga became a reality by chance. It seems that Mr. H.C. (Cargie) Rymill, an Australian aristocrat and well known-golfer, traveled by tram rather than the train to Henley Beach. Along this journey in 1922 he saw a "For Sale" sign on a tract of swamp land that also had an area of ancient sand dunes. On closer inspection he recognized that he had discovered an ideal site for a golf course. By 1923 he had designed the first nine holes, added three more holes by New Year's and by June 1924, the completed eighteen holes were open for play. The name Kooyonga was given to this golf club as he was under the impression that the word was an aboriginal word meaning "plenty sand, plenty water". It turns out that the translation means something slightly different but the name has stuck.

Kooyonga is not a long course; in fact none of the par fours measure over 440 yards, and two of the three par fives are reachable in two by the long hitters. The layout meanders through abundant natural trees which define narrow fairways and well protected, smallish greens. Despite looking flat from outside the paddock, the course has interesting elevation changes. The terrain is a series of rises and hollows upon which some wonderful golf holes have been designed. The outgoing nine rotates clockwise on the outside of the property, followed by the incoming nine rotating counterclockwise inside the former, but only returning to the clubhouse at eighteen. When I visited in 2008 the new clubhouse was not quite finished.

What was so impressive to me was that every hole seemed to be isolated in its own natural surrounds with each green framed by red sand bunkers that extend to the green's edge. They provide a superb defensive mechanism for any shot that is neither exact nor on line. A perfect example is the fourth green: after a blind tee shot over a sandy ridge, one is faced with one of the most inspiring second shots in Australia. Any misdirected shot, a slice, as us duffers hit, or a hook will roll off the green and into an adjacent bunker. (Figure 73)

Kooyonga has been rated consistently in the top fifteen courses in Australia since ratings became popular. It has hosted five Australian Opens, three Australian Amateur Championships and numerous South Australian Opens. I have not listed it in my list of favorites, but if you travel to South Australia do not miss playing this course.

Figure 73. The fourth hole at Kooyonga framed by
bunkers and native trees

Sydney, Australia

Sydney was our last stop in Australia and a mistake
we made is that we only allowed three days to visit,
see the sights and play at New South Wales and
Royal Sydney. I immediately recognized this error
and canceled my round at Royal Sydney in favor of a
day at the beach. We spent a rushed morning touring
the Royal Opera House and really could have spent
two days there, easily. It is one of the most
impressive, examples of modern architecture in the
world. There were no performances there during our
visit: another mistake we made. If I go back I will
spend the better part of a week in Sydney and not
play golf, and definitely plan the visit around a

performance here. It's like trying to visit New York City in three days; it just cannot be done.

New South Wales Golf Club, La Perouse, Sydney, NSW, Australia

New South Wales Golf Club is beautifully situated on the northern headland of Botany Bay, flanked by the rugged cliffs of Henry Head and the headland of Cape Banks. The setting couldn't be more perfect. Bounded on three sides by water, it has many of the characteristics of a true links course. The location is perfect: in the Sydney suburb of La Perouse, twenty minutes from the Sydney City Center. Botany Bay is of further historical significance, as Captain James Cook's expedition first made landfall here after sailing from the UK, first to New Zealand and on to the eastern coast of Australia. He found a fresh water spring on the southern headland directly adjacent to the current location of the seventeenth tee. Furthermore, the first fleet of British convicts and settlers who were, in fact, the first white inhabitants, arrived to the shores of Botany in 1788, only eight years after his initial discovery.

The Club was founded in the fall of 1926 and visited by Dr. Alister MacKenzie six months later, during which time he outlined the original course routing and the bunkering plan. The uncompleted course was open for play in June of 1928, but the stock market crash in 1929 delayed MacKenzie's completed design until 1932. The design completion of the bunkers and alterations of the routing were done by E. L. (Eric) Apperly, who is also credited with designing the wonderful four par three's here. This work was done from 1932-37 and restoration done again in 1949-51, after World War II. Three other architectural firms have had a hand in restoring greens, tees and bunkers beginning in the mid 1980's. They are Thomson & Wolveridge, Newton, Grant & Spencer, and Norman & Harrison.

The entire course offers magnificent views of the ocean from a stunning series of holes built around, over and through hills and valleys that lead to the rugged coast. This quote from MacKenzie sums it up better than I could: "At Sydney, I made an entirely new course for the New South Wales Golf Club (NSW) at a place called La Perouse. This presents, I think, more spectacular views than any other place I know with the possible exception of the new Cypress Point Golf Club in California." The turf is composed of couch grass on undulating fairways and small bent grass greens. The layout is very exposed to the Tasman Sea, with its highly unpredictable winds; scoring here is very difficult.

My arrival at NSW Golf Club was rushed and confusing as they had no caddies and the course was crowded. I was paired with a couple from California; I have always called this situation an M & M. (i.e. Mr. & Ms.) Often traveling with only my wife, who rarely plays, I have frequently encountered this scenario. It's my experience that an M & M situation usually means the wife or lady hits the ball better than the man, but in all circumstances neither has a clue as to golf course etiquette or pace of play. Also, I have failed to discuss this earlier, but Australia was in the fourth year of a five year drought. Any course without a water retention pond was playing very firm and fast, so playing without a caddie to give us the line and warnings was frustrating as we all would hit blind shots that sailed into impossible rough and we all had a disproportionate number of lost balls. There were five blind shots in the first nine holes alone. Not good!

One unusual factor regarding the layout is that there are two areas, both elevated, that have a heavy concentration of holes ending and starting in these locations, like spokes on a wagon wheel. Augusta National calls these areas "spectator viewing sites", but as we discuss the layout here, I will call them concentration areas. The first tee is located directly outside the doors entering and exiting from the clubhouse. The second is a long par three with a blind tee shot to a small green, and the third is yet another blind tee shot to a sharp dogleg left par four. All three of us blasted over the dogleg into heavy scrub resulting in three lost balls, primarily because we had no idea of the line we should take. The long par four fourth ends at the top of the headland and its green is located in the first concentration area discussed above. This area is also occupied by the fifth tee, the seventh green, the eighth tee, the twelfth green and lastly the thirteenth tee. The fifth tumbles down from a wide fairway to the edge of Botany Bay.

The dramatic par three sixth is probably the signature hole and interesting because it was not included in MacKenzie's plan. There is speculation that this land was not available in 1926. The design of the sixth was left to Eric Apperly who placed the tee on a rocky outcrop behind the fifth green. The shot demands a carry over the ocean to a small sloping green back on the top of the headland. Apperly also redesigned MacKenzie's seventh and eighth to become the monster par five eighth headed back toward the center of the course and ending up in the second concentration area. This area also includes the ninth tee, the tenth green, and finally the eleventh tee and green on this short par three, guarded circumferentially by four deep bunkers.

Similar to the fifth, the thirteenth sweeps back down to the headland and ocean, followed by the short par four fourteenth which runs parallel to the coast and requires a demanding tee shot across a ravine filled with scrub and tea trees. The fifteenth and sixteenth are parallel, long par fours with the former headed inland and the latter's green on the coast. (Figure 74)

Figure 74. View looking back at the headland and fourteenth green from NSW's sixteenth green

The short par three seventeenth's green is very exposed to the wind and elements and usually demands an accurate 150 yard shot, while the 528 par five eighteenth ends at a punchbowl green below the clubhouse.

I must say that the views of the ocean and rocky coast are spectacular, but the blind shots and overall conditioning of the course has me ranking it ninety-seventh in my list of favorites.

Ranking of the nine courses I played in Australia and those in my list of favorites.

1. Royal Melbourne Golf Club (West Course), # 10
2. Barnbougle Dunes Golf Club, # 25
3. Kingston Heath Golf Club, # 47
4. The Victoria Golf Club, # 84
5. New South Wales Golf Club, # 97
6. Royal Melbourne (East) Golf Club
7. The Metropolitan Golf Club
8. Kooyonga Golf Club
9. Royal Adelaide Golf Club

Sample itinerary for a golfing trip to Australia

The flights from the US typically leave from LAX or another city on the west coast in the late evening. Doing that, you arrive in Melbourne in the morning, but lose a day going west. I'm assuming you arrive in Melbourne refreshed enough to get right on playing. If not you can spend the day of arrival resting or, as we did, sightseeing.

1. Arrival day. If you miss playing either one of these clubs, it is not a great loss, but play Metropolitan or if you can arrange it, Yarra Yarra, which is an exclusive club.
2. Play Victoria Golf Club. You should stay in downtown Melbourne as it's not far to the sandbelt courses.
3. Start off at Royal Melbourne's East Course on day three
4. Play Royal Melbourne West Course. I'm assuming playing one round per day, but if you can play two rounds a day, you can shorten your trip or leave more time to explore.
5. Play Kingston Heath. This course along with Royal Melbourne West are "must play" venues. Travel south to the Mornington Peninsula and The National Golf Club
6. Play The Old Course here. It's a Robert Trent Jones, Jr. design. You are still on your sixth day here.
7. There are two other courses here: The Ocean Course with spectacular ocean views and/or Moonah, a Greg Norman design.
8. After a week I would definitely take a day off and fly to Tasmania.
9. Play Barnbougle Dunes Course.
10. Play Barnbougle Lost Farm Course.

11. Since you are almost at the southern end of the earth, I would play one of these two courses again before loading up for the long trip home.

Well, we've come to the end of this book. I'm sure the reader can tell as least three things about me.
1. I wanted to write this book to give back something to the golfing world as it has meant so much to me and my life.
2. I'm totally addicted to playing and reading about golf.
3. I have the golf gene. In "Links" Magazine, James A. Frank defines this key trait as one who "must play the world's best courses".

My goal was to help the reader explore, in print, both the heralded and the not so heralded golf destinations across the ponds. I sincerely hope that goal has been achieved.

"This book is his labor of love" is what Tom Fazio insightfully said. He is so right!

Acknowledgements

First and foremost I would to thank my wife Faye T. Kitchens for putting up with me during this two year process. She can and did spell hundreds of words for me. She also proof read the book several times. Secondly, I am indebted to my IT associate Matthew W. Long whose overall help was invaluable and without which I would never have completed this endeavor.

Thirdly, I appreciate the help of Adam Messix, PGA Head Pro at Headwaters Golf Club, Tim Boeve, PGA Head Pro at The Reserve at Lake Koewee, Eric Peterson, PGA Head Pro at Greenville Country Club's Chanticleer Course, Karl Stefka, PGA Head Pro at GCC's Riverside Course, Pete Mathews, PGA Wade Hampton Golf Club's Director of Golf, Shannon Howell, PGA Head Pro at The Country Club of Sapphire Valley. All spent countless hours advising me, encouraging me and reading several chapters in the early and later stages of this book.

Thank you to my good friend Middleton (Mid) Parker who started this project with the question: Just how many golf courses have you played?

Lastly I am deeply indebted to two friends, Tom Fazio and Ian Bamford, who wrote the foreword and preface to this book.

All of the photographs here were taken by the author or his son, Dr. G. Gray Kitchens, Jr.